# Liberators

*Walking in the Victory of Christ*

Josiah Greaver

*Liberators*
Walking in the Victory of Christ
By Josiah Greaver


Copyright © 2023 Josiah Greaver

All rights reserved under International Copyright Law. Contents and/or cover may not be reproduced in whole or in part, except for brief quotations in critical reviews or articles, without the expressed written consent of the publisher.

Unless otherwise noted, all scriptures are taken from THE HOLY BIBLE, NEW INTERNATIONAL VERSION®, NIV® Copyright © 1973, 1978, 1984, 2011 by Biblica, Inc.® Used by permission. All rights reserved worldwide.

Scripture quotations marked (NLT) are taken from the Holy Bible, New Living Translation, copyright ©1996, 2004, 2015 by Tyndale House Foundation. Used by permission of Tyndale House Publishers, Inc., Carol Stream, Illinois 60188. All rights reserved.

Scripture quotations marked KJV are from *The Kings James Version* of the Bible, public domain.

Scripture quotations taken from the Amplified® Bible (AMPC), Copyright © 1954, 1958, 1962, 1964, 1965, 1987 by The Lockman Foundation. Used by permission. www.Lockman.org.

All uppercase text in verses of scripture are added by the author for the purpose of emphasis.

Published by Josiah Greaver

ISBN: 979-218-20666-6

Printed in the United States of America

# DEDICATION

This book is dedicated to my Savior Jesus Christ. Without His abundance of love and blessing I would have nothing. I also dedicate this to Alyssa, my wife, best friend and co-laborer.

# CONTENTS

| | | |
|---|---|---|
| | Dedication | Pg. ii |
| Intro | Looking Unto Jesus | Pg. 4 |
| 1 | Christ in You | Pg. 13 |
| 2 | Having the Mind of Christ | Pg. 27 |
| 3 | Faith to Be and Do | Pg. 38 |
| 4 | Living Righteously | Pg. 59 |
| 5 | Living with Healing Power | Pg. 79 |
| 6 | Living Out Financial Prosperity | Pg. 105 |
| 7 | Understanding Job and the Goodness of God | Pg. 127 |
| 8 | Lessons from Job | Pg. 144 |
| 9 | Understanding Suffering and Paul's Thorn | Pg. 163 |
| | End Notes | Pg. 179 |

## INTRODUCTION

# LOOKING UNTO JESUS

One of the most common phrases in Christianity is: What Would Jesus Do? If you grew up in church in the 90's and early 2000's you probably owned a WWJD wristband. Now, you may argue that the phrase is a bit cliché. And maybe it is. But you can't argue that it's not a good one. Obviously, we Christians should strive very hard to be like Jesus. As 1 John 2:6 tells us, **"Whoever claims to live in him must live as Jesus did."**

But in my experience, how to go about that isn't always quite so apparent. That is, a lot of believers only have it half-right. If that.

Growing up in church, I heard a lot about the Jesus of love. I heard a lot about being compassionate and patient and forgiving. But when I started to pull about my Bible and read it for myself, and began questioning things, I realized there was a missing piece to the Jesus puzzle. A major piece.

Jesus was loving, yes. But I challenge you to ask yourself: does love define in full who Jesus was? And then with our WWJD understanding, does love define in full who we're supposed to be?

## JESUS THE LIBERATOR

Marking the start of His earthly ministry, Jesus stood in the temple and read from Isaiah concerning Himself and His mission:

**"The Spirit of the Lord is on me, because he has anointed me to proclaim good news to the poor. He has sent me to proclaim freedom for the prisoners and recovery of sight for the blind, to set the oppressed free, to proclaim the year of the Lord's favor."**

Luke 4:18-19

Jesus proclaimed that He was anointed by God through the Holy Spirit to be what we might call a liberator—that is, to set people free from the bondage of suffering, sickness and sin.

Just a few verses later He is out and about doing these very things. In verses 33-35 Jesus casts an evil spirit out of a man. In verse 38 he heals a woman suffering a high fever. Then verse 40 says, **"At sunset, the people brought to Jesus all who had various kinds of sickness, and laying his hands on each one, healed them"** (Luke 4:40).

So Jesus wasn't only full of love, He was a liberator. If we are honest theologically, we must accept that Jesus' earthly ministry consisted of more interactions involving some sort of healing or deliverance than extending love, mercy or forgiveness. He spent most of His time living in this function as a liberator.

Over the past several years I have noticed a lopsided approach to how ministries preach Jesus. Much has been said about the Jesus of love while little has been said about the Jesus of power to set people free. In turn, this has affected who the Church—namely, the individual believer—has become: what he believes, how he thinks of himself, and what he does. Because of the emphasis on love, the believer stands with arms wide open to accept the sinner and the broken. Yet because of a lack of emphasis on power, he stands incapable of ministering by the anointing of the Holy Spirit to see set free those very people who are oppressed, sick or bound by sin. So he is compassionate in vain.

In fact, the Jesus of power has become somewhat of a fantasy in many Christian circles. We've been told that Jesus is a comforter, an anchor in the storm, although when Jesus was in storms He *stopped* them, not comforted people through them (Mark 4:35-41). Radio stations broadcast songs that portray a God who doesn't move the mountains or part the waters, that He just gives us the strength to endure, although Jesus promised *we* could speak to mountains and command them to move (Mark 11:23). Even in terms of sin many churches have become referral stations for those with addictions and issues, pointing them to counselors and AA-like groups for "help" instead of to the Lord for deliverance.

I've heard it preached, "We don't love God for what He does but for who He is." That sounds nice and religious, but who He is *is* a Healer, Deliverer, Savior, Provider and Redeemer. Those aren't ideals or nice names we came up with for God, they are descriptions of His Divine Personality.

In other words, who He is and what He does go hand-in-hand. They're two sides of the same coin. When the woman subject to bleeding for 12 years pushed through the crowd to touch Jesus for healing, she got healing. He didn't rebuke her for wanting the healing more than the Healer because it's one and the same. That's evidenced in the fact that He wasn't even aiming to heal her. He was simply walking through her town. She touched Him. And in touching Him, she touched healing.

My intent here is not to downplay love. Love is vital and should be an utmost priority. We must understand, however, that love does not replace the need for spiritual power and authority.

Genuine love necessitates power. It was Jesus' love for people that drove Him to be a liberator. Matthew 14:14 tells us, **"When Jesus landed and saw a large crowd, he had compassion on them and healed their sick."** Truly loving people isn't merely feeling sorry for them, it is healing or delivering them by God's power.

## WE ARE CALLED TO BE LIBERATORS

If Jesus is a liberator, and He is, why don't we see more miracles today? Why aren't more people being healed of sickness like when Jesus was on earth? Why are so many even in the Church struggling with sin when we're supposed to be free from its power?

Jesus hasn't changed. Scripture tells us, **"Jesus Christ is the same yesterday and today and forever"** (Hebrews 13:8). He wants to do the same things now that He did while on earth. So why?

The answer is simple: Jesus ascended into Heaven and is no longer on earth; therefore, His work as liberator can only continue if believers carry it out. The Bible says that Christ is the head and the Church is His body (Colossians 1:18). The head decides what to do, and the body carries it out. Likewise, we who are Christ's body are responsible for carrying out the Lord's will.

To be frank: miracles aren't happening at large because believers aren't performing them. Granted, I see healings and miracles about every week now that I believe the right things and am in the right ministry circle. But people outside of that, which I would argue is most of Western Christianity at this point, don't see let alone perform the miraculous.

If you are one of those Western Christianity believers, good. I wrote this book just for you because I used to be like you. Just hang in there and read this, for I whole-heartedly believe God is about to upend your life in the best way possible.

If you think how I did, you probably *believe* in miracles. You simply believe that it's up to God if they happen or not. "If God wants it done, it will happen." You think that way and you pray that way.

Well, you couldn't be more biblically incorrect. You are not properly understanding God's sovereignty or will.

God's will for an individual does not automatically happen. For example, although it is God's will for everyone to be saved (2 Peter 3:9), people can choose hell by refusing Jesus (John 5:40). People aren't automatically saved simply because God wants them to be. This principle works in reverse, as well. For example, it's *not* God's will for people to be murdered, yet people murder others every day.

In order for God's will to save, heal and deliver to manifest, we must align ourselves with it. We must believe it and act on it.

There is not a single instance in the Bible where God willed a certain thing to be done and accomplished it without using a person. He used Moses to deliver Israel out of Egyptian slavery, David to deliver Israel from the Philistines, He even sent Jesus as a *man* to redeem mankind. God has always used people to accomplish His will on the earth and He always will. Therefore, we must align ourselves with who He has called us to be in order to see the lost saved, sick healed and broken delivered.

Who has God called us to be? Before He ascended into Heaven, Jesus told us. He called us to be just like Him: liberators.

**"Very truly I tell you, whoever believes in me will do the works I have been doing, and they will do even greater things than these, because I am going to the Father."**

John 14:12

**"As the Father has sent me, so I am sending you."**

John 20:21 (NLT)

**"He said to them, 'Go into all the world and preach the gospel to all creation. Whoever believes and is baptized will be saved, but whoever does not believe will be condemned. And these signs will accompany those who believe: In my name they will drive out demons; they will speak in new tongues; they will pick up snakes with their hands; and when they drink deadly poison, it will not hurt them at all; they will place their hands**

**on sick people, and they will get well.'"**

Mark 16:17-18

Don't miss it! Go back and read those scriptures again if you have to. Jesus commissioned us to do the same things He did. We are sent just as He was sent. So how was he sent? As a liberator. We are called to be liberators. We are not called *just* to love people, we are called to liberate people by the power of God.

This call to be a liberator is for every believer. Jesus did not say "some who believe in me" will do greater works than Him or heal the sick. He said "any" who believe. That means you and I. There is not a single instance in scripture where we find that the power of the Holy Spirit was limited to the 12 apostles or confined to a time limit after His resurrection. The book of Acts accounts both men and women who flowed in supernatural power who were not apostles: Stephen, Timothy, Philip's daughters and the like.

Since we are called to be liberators, we are not called to be strugglers. It is the will of the devil to make believers captive to the very things God called us to deliver in others, such as sickness, poverty and sin. That's because Satan is a thief who comes to steal, kill and destroy (John 10:10). And if he can stop us from living in victory, he'll stop us from living as liberators for others. So let us not fall prey to those who suppose we must struggle with sin, or who suppose that sickness is just an unfortunate part of life. God's will for our lives is us to be liberators, to be us praying for the sick and performing miracles, not being in need of them.

## PURPOSE OF THIS BOOK

Hebrews 12:2 (KJV) declares, **"Looking unto Jesus the author and finisher of our faith."** Jesus is our example to follow. He's who we look at. He has established the pattern for our faith. Every question about life *can and must* be answered through the lens of Christ, whether it's a matter of healing, righteousness, joy or prosperity.

This book will look at who Jesus was (and is) but will more specifically look to how we can *be* who Jesus is. In his book, *Concerning Spiritual Gifts*, Donald Gee writes, "Much stress is laid upon [Jesus'] teaching, but with little indication as to how men are to receive the power to follow it.[1]" Merely knowing the life and miracles of Jesus does us no good if we remain clueless as to what we must do to replicate them. Unlocking the "how" is of great importance.

Therefore, in this book we will discover and apply the truth from scripture that shows us how to be like Christ: how to live like Him, think like Him and have the faith to do what He did. In order to be as specific and relevant as possible, we will discuss what that looks like in three of the most important facets of life: righteousness, health and finances.

Additionally, this book will answer some of the most common questions that arise when discussing matters of victory, healing, deliverance and prosperity. Because of bad teachings through the years, much light needs shed on the story of Job, the goodness of God, Paul's thorn, and the true meaning of "suffering for Christ."

It is time for the Church to arise and be not only Christ's love but also His power. May you walk in victory and truly live like Jesus as a result of the truths from scripture that are revealed in this book!

## CHAPTER 1

# CHRIST IN YOU

During His time on earth, Jesus was a liberator. He set people free from demonic oppression, healed the sick, raised the dead and conquered sin. By dying on the cross, He finalized His victory for us. Colossians 2:15 says, **"And having disarmed the powers and authorities, he made a public spectacle of them, triumphing over them by the cross."**

We refer to His victory as the supremacy of Christ. Colossians 1 contains perhaps the most powerful passage on His supremacy in the New Testament. Yet no matter how great Jesus' victory is and no matter many times we talk about it, His triumph over Satan in itself means nothing if we don't realize how it applies to us.

After his revelation about the supremacy Jesus, the Apostle Paul continues in Colossians 1 by saying he is called **"to present to you the word of God in its FULLNESS"** (Colossians 1:25). In other words, there was more that needed said and understood within the subject of Christ's supremacy. He goes on to say, **"To them God has chosen to make known among the Gentiles the glorious** riches of this mystery, **WHICH IS CHRIST IN YOU, the hope of glory"** (Colossians 1:27). The New Living Translation presents it even clearer: **"Christ lives in you."** So, the revelation about the supremacy of Christ is only *full*, or complete, once the believer understands that Christ lives in him.

In Galatians 2:20, Paul provides some basic insight into what this means, saying, **"I have been crucified with Christ and I no longer live, but Christ lives in me."** Once a person confesses faith in Jesus as the Son of God who was crucified and raised back to life, His life becomes his life. Jesus comes and lives in him, for the Bible says we receive the Spirit of Christ (Romans 8:9-11).

As a result, the life Jesus lived on earth and everything He was able to do—from living sinless to being a liberator for people—becomes our life. We become able to live exactly as He lived because He lives in us. We receive a victorious life.

## VICTORY OF THE BELIEVER

The Christ, the Anointed One of God who conquered all powers and dominion, lives inside the believer! Take a moment to say it, "Christ lives in me." Because He lived a victorious life, we can live victorious lives—over sin, no matter the temptation; over sickness, no matter the doctor's report; over lack, no matter how great the need. 2 Corinthians 2:14 (KJV) says, **"Now thanks be unto God, which always causeth us to triumph in Christ."** Christ in us causes us to *always* triumph, which means in victory after victory.

Let us make this personal:

Everything Jesus wasn't I don't have to be. Was He sinful? No! Then I do not have to be because He lives in me! Or is there a temptation the devil can bring that's greater than who lives in me (1 John 4:4)? By no means!

Was He sick? No! Then I don't have to be. Or could cancer cells exist in Jesus? Impossible!

Did He ever lack? No! He multiplied food to feed thousands (Matthew 14:13-21) and caused fish to produce money from their mouths (Matthew 17:24-27) for goodness sake! So neither must I lack.

Everything Jesus was and did I can do because He lives in me. I can live completely sin free. I can heal the sick. I can even raise the dead! Anything is possible for me because Jesus is living and working through me.

Think again of Jesus' words in John 14:12: "**Very truly I tell you, whoever believes in me will do the works I have been doing, and they will do even greater things than these, because I am going to the Father.**" He was not being metaphorical. He was being literal. He fully expected us to heal the sick, raise the dead and perform miracles.

Western Christianity's preaching too often fails to move beyond the supremacy of Christ into the victory of the believer. It gets stuck on:

"God can do it."

"God's in control."

"Let go and let God."

I once came across a minister who said, "Remember, whatever is over your head is still under His feet." Let's analyze this for a moment in light of "Christ in you." The Bible tells us, **"And God raised us up with Christ and seated us with him in the heavenly realms in Christ Jesus"** (Ephesians 2:6). This means we are on the same plane as Christ—not in heaven one day, now. We are "raised" not "will be raised." So if we're on the same plane as Jesus, what is under His feet is under our feet. In order for it to be under *His* feet it must be under *our* feet!

The revelation of Christ in you doesn't just mean that Jesus is victorious, it means that we too are victorious. Jesus didn't win all the power and take it to heaven for Himself. No! The Bible calls us **"more than conquerors through him who loved us"** (Romans 8:37). What is more than a conqueror? It is one who receives the prize from someone else who did the fighting.

For example, imagine a boxer who after several rounds defeats his opponent. After receiving the prize money, he returns home only to have his wife swipe the check out of his hands while smiling and saying, "I'll take that!" The wife is the "more than the conqueror." She didn't have to fight but she reaped the reward.

That is what Christ did for us! He fought and won the battle so we don't have to. We don't have to battle sickness, Jesus fought and won. We don't have to battle sin, Jesus fought and won. We don't have to battle financial lack. Jesus won. We simply walk in His victory as more than conquerors. My friends, we might be in this world, but we are not of this world. We are above it. It cannot conqueror us, for Christ lives in us.

If we are in a place of need or sickness, God can certainly do something about our situation, but it will come by God working through *us*. Ephesians 3:20 tells us, **"Now to him who is able to do immeasurably more than all we ask or imagine, according to his power that is AT WORK WITHIN US."** Where is His power at work? In us. Immeasurably more can only be done by God's power through us.

When people suppose, "it will happen if God wants it to happen," they take themselves out of the equation. His power is not merely working, it's at work *in us*. We can't be taken out of the equation. So the question is not "if it's His will," but if we'll submit to His will and consecrate ourselves to carry His power.

Remember this: God is sovereign, but He's put you in control. Jesus tells us in Matthew 16:19, **"I will give you the keys of the kingdom of heaven; whatever you bind on earth will be bound in heaven, and whatever you loose on earth will be loosed in heaven."** In other words, what we allow, God will allow and what we forbid, God will forbid. So what we don't do won't get done, and what we allow will never be conquered. If we think that sickness or lack is "just a part of life," God won't forbid it because we're not forbidding it. We're just letting it remain, not opposing the attack of the enemy in faith. We might be submitted to God, but we're not resisting the enemy (James 4:7).

Luke 10:18-19 tells us that we've been given authority **"to overcome all power of the enemy; nothing will harm you."** He was speaking to the disciples at the time, but His victory on the cross and resurrection applies these words to us now. *All* power has been given to us. Jesus isn't hogging it. We have the power to say to the mountain, **"Go, throw yourself into the sea"** (Mark 11:23) and it will happen. We have the authority to say, "Cancer, I command you to come out of her body in Jesus name!"

Since He gave all power to us, there is none leftover for the devil. Most Christians live paranoid of what the devil will do in their lives. They go around saying things like, "I hope I don't get that sickness going around." They think they are subject to his evil plans and schemes that destroy lives.

The Bible says, **"For he has rescued us from the dominion of darkness and brought us into the kingdom of the Son he loves"** (Colossians 1:13). We are no longer under the dominion of Satan. We are not subject to his evil plans and schemes to destroy our lives. We don't just have to put up and try to cope with the bad things he sends our way. Rather, we have power in Christ to frustrate the devil's plans. Instead of fearing and hoping we don't get sick, we can go around healing the sick (Mark 16:15-18). Instead of hoping we have enough money to pay our bills, we can be such big givers that others shout in praise to the Lord (2 Corinthians 9:12-13).

## DEFEAT IS DEFEATED

Allow it to begin settling firmly in your mind: we no longer need to struggle.

Religion is full of unbiblical catchphrases like, "God never promised us an easy life, just that it would be worth it." As wonderfully spiritual as this sounds, Jesus tells us the exact opposite: **"Take my yoke upon you and learn from me…For my yoke is**

**EASY and my burden is LIGHT"** (Matthew 11:29-20). He said our life serving Him would be easy and light. How? Because He lives in us and we have access to His power.

Only someone blinded by religion would say, "With God I have everything and all power," and then proceed to act like they have nothing and that life is a struggle. It makes no sense. We need to make up our minds. Either we have everything or nothing at all. Either we have God's power or we don't. And if we do have it, there's no other choice than for life to be easy and light.

Think about it: We're serving God, not Satan. If God was the thief, murderer and destroyer, it would make sense to think life would be hard. But God is good and Satan is the oppressor (Acts 10:38).

On top of that, most of the problems people have are direct consequences of sinful decisions. Divorce, sexual immorality, lying, drugs, alcoholism, jealousy, and greed are some of the top problem-causers today. That's what the Bible means when it says, **"the wages of sin is death"** (Romans 6:23) and **"Troubles chases sinners, while blessings reward the righteous**  (Proverbs 13:21 NLT). And since believers are redeemed from that way of life, they are not doing those things that cause people to live under such turmoil. Holy living doesn't give you sexually transmitted diseases. Being faithful to each other in marriage isn't a cause for divorce. Paying tithes and giving to the poor doesn't make you poor. Righteous living eliminates most of life's suffering! In fact, it causes blessings to find us. 1 Timothy 4:8 (NLT) tells us, **"Physical training is good, but training for godliness is much better, promising benefits in this life and in** the life to come."

One may say, "But Jesus promised us trouble." So I ask: And where do you find that He said we must be defeated by it? Nowhere. That verse about trouble doesn't end with Jesus just promising trouble and wishing us the best of luck. The full verse actually says, **"In this world you will have trouble. But take heart! I have overcome the world"** (John 16:33).

What does "I have overcome the world" mean? From what we now know about the revelation of Christ in you, it must mean something changes *for us*, because Christ didn't just win the victory for Himself. The AMPC translation sheds light on what Jesus meant, saying, **"For I have overcome the world. [I have deprived it of power to harm you and have conquered it for you.]"** The trouble cannot harm us because Jesus overcame it and gave us the victory!

Regardless of what comes our way, we are able to overcome. No sickness, hardship or lack the devil can raise up against us is allowed to prosper. Isaiah 54:17 (KJV) tells us, **"No weapon that is formed against thee shall prosper…this is the heritage of the servants of the Lord."** Likewise, Psalm 34:19 says, **"The righteous person may have many troubles, but the LORD delivers him from them all; he protects all his bones, not one of them will be broken."** We don't deny the reality of the devil, but we firmly resist the idea that he can harm or defeat us, for God protects and delivers us. God doesn't comfort us through the troubles, He has given us power in Christ to put them to naught. The victory is ours.

Evangelist Jonathan Shuttlesworth says it like this: it's scriptural to be challenged, but it's unscriptural to be defeated. God's people are never defeated in the Bible. Did an ocean stop Moses and the Israelites from crossing to the other side? Did the giants in the land of Canaan stop Israel from possessing it? Did Goliath stop David? These and more all answer a resounding, "No!" And if all of those were *before* Christ, how much more should we continue in victory *after* Christ when Christ is living in us!

## ALIGNING WITH OUR IDENTITY

How we identify in life is important because a person will live according to who they think they are. Someone that identifies as a businessman or woman will think, talk and dress as such. Or someone that thinks they are worthless and unloved will struggle with depression and may commit suicide. That's what the Bible means when it says, **"For as he thinketh in his heart, so is he"** (Proverbs 23:7 KJV).

Christians fail to live in the victory identity we have in Christ because they have their identity mixed up. They identify as someone who will never amount to anything, so they never do. They identify as someone who is sick, so they struggle with sickness. They identify as a recovering alcoholic, so they struggle against alcoholism.

There is only One with who we should be identifying and that's Jesus. The Bible says, **"Do not conform to the pattern of this world, but be transformed by the renewing of your mind. Then you will be able to test and approve what God's will is--his good, pleasing and perfect will"** (Romans 12:2). Don't identify with the suffering and defeat that's in the world. Instead, we must align our thinking with who God says we are and what God says we can do.

The late Pastor John Osteen used to begin every sermon with the audience wide declaration: "This is my Bible. I am who it says I am. I have what it says I have. I can do what it says I can do…" It does not matter how the world identifies us. It doesn't what our families, friends or coworkers think of us. What does matter is who God says we are! And that is how we must align our thinking.

We align our minds with the victory identity we have in Christ by taking our thoughts captive and make them obedient to Christ. 2 Corinthians 10:5 tells us, **"We demolish arguments and every pretension that sets itself up against the knowledge of God, and we take captive every thought to make it obedient to Christ."** This means resisting every thought that contradicts the Word of God and replacing it with what God has actually said. In doing so, we stay in faith and keep pressing forward to victory in that area of our lives.

When the thought comes that we'll get diagnosed with heart disease just like our father and his father, we say, "No! This is what the Word says. This is who I am and what I have in Jesus." We command our thoughts to be God's thoughts, and in so doing we stay in faith.

When the thought comes that we're still an alcoholic, we declare, "Who the Son sets free is free indeed. I am free. That is who I am." We command our thoughts to be God's thoughts, and in so doing we stay in faith.

As we align our identity with the victory identity we have in

Christ, we will in no time see the results of having fully grasped God's will for us!

## ACTIVATION BY THE ANOINTING

Despite being the Son of God, Jesus did not perform a single miracle or healing until after He received the anointing of the Holy Spirit. It activated the power of God upon Him. Jesus declared this in Luke 4:18-19 saying, **"The Spirit of the Lord is on me, because he has anointed me to…"**

The term "anointing" originates in the Old Testament and meant getting oil poured on one's head or body to mark a setting apart for special use by God (1 Kings 19:16, Exodus 40:15, Leviticus 16:32, 1 Samuel 9:16). It was symbolic but also caused a manifestation of God's Spirit to come on the individual.

Instead of being anointed by a natural substance, Jesus' anointing was supernatural by the Holy Spirit Himself. We read of this event in John 1:32-34:

**"Then John gave this testimony: "I saw the Spirit come down from heaven as a dove and remain on him. And I myself did not know him, but the one who sent me to baptize with water told me, 'The man on whom you see the Spirit come down and remain is the one who will baptize with the Holy Spirit.' I have seen and I testify that this is God's Chosen One."**

John 1:32-34

Notice twice the passage said the Holy Spirit "remained" on Jesus. It was after this point that His ministry began (also see Luke 3:21-23) and where He began to perform signs and wonders.

As with Jesus, although we are children of God with Jesus living on the inside of us, an activation from the Holy Spirit is necessary for us to carry God's power in our lives to be liberators. This is called the baptism of the Holy Spirit (Acts 19:1-3).

How do we receive the baptism of the Holy Spirit? Jesus' anointing set Him apart to be a distributor to us the very Spirit and power He received. We read in the passage above from John, **"The man on whom you see the Spirit come down and remain IS THE ONE WHO WILL BAPTIZE WITH THE HOLY SPIRIT."** And in another place, **"He will baptize you with the Holy Spirit and fire"** (Luke 3:16).

So Jesus was to give us a baptism—meaning full submersion—in the Holy Spirit so that the power of God would be activated on our lives. Jesus said:

**"But very truly I tell you, it is for your good that I am going away. Unless I go away, the Advocate will not come to you; but if I go, I will send him to you."**

John 16:7

**"But you will receive power when the Holy Spirit comes on you; and you will be my witnesses in Jerusalem, and in all Judea and Samaria, and to the ends of the earth."**

Acts 1:8

Jesus told the disciples that they would receive power to *be* witnesses. That's different than going out *to* witness. Anyone has the ability to go out *to* witness about Jesus, but we need the power and fire of the Holy Spirit to *be* witnesses. Our very lives are to be testimonies of God's power and love.

Look at what the Bible records about Peter after he received the baptism of the Spirit. He became an attractive force for the Lord. It says that **"people brought the sick into the streets and laid them on beds and mats so that at least Peter's shadow might fall on some of them as he passed by"** (Acts 5:15). People knew something was different about him compared to others. They knew God was alive on the inside of him in such a way that if they could just get close to him they would be healed or delivered. People flocked to Jesus in the same way. How did this happen? Receiving the baptism of the Holy Spirit caused Peter to *be* a witness. He didn't just go out to witness, he became one.

You can be a witness, as well. The same baptism of the Holy Spirit is for you, for every believer. Jesus said in John 7:38-39:

**"Whoever believes in me, as Scripture has said, rivers of living water will flow from within them." By this he meant the Spirit, whom those who believed in him were later to receive. Up to that time the Spirit had not been given, since Jesus had not yet been glorified."**

Jesus said "whoever." That means you and I. He said it would be like a river of living water flowing from you. When you go to work, your coworkers will feel the presence of God flowing from you. When you walk in a hospital to visit the sick, God's river of life will begin healing bodies. Every demonic force oppressing someone must flee when you are near.

On one instance when I was preaching, there was a woman who needed prayer for having seizures. I felt in my spirit that it was a demonic spirit causing her attacks. As I went to place my hand on her head to pray, I said, "I command the evil spirit giving you seizures to leave you at once in Jesus name!" But before I was actually able to put my hand on her head, she fell hard to the ground as if stepped on by a massive foot, and she shook violently as the evil spirit left her. The Holy Spirit flowing through me was so much greater than the demonic spirit that I didn't even have to touch her for her to be delivered. It left easily by words and proximity.

Step forward into the fullness of Christ in you. Receive the baptism of the Holy Spirit now. Lift your hands and say, "Jesus, baptize me with the Holy Spirit and fire as you promised you would."

*CHAPTER 2*

# HAVING THE MIND OF CHRIST

Jesus always knew God's will. He always knew who God was and who God said He was. Jesus always knew God's plans, which meant always knowing what He needed to do. John 5:19-20 tells us:

**"Jesus gave them this answer: 'Very truly I tell you, the Son can do nothing by himself; he can do only what he sees his Father doing, because whatever the Father does the Son also does. For the Father loves the Son and shows him all he does. Yes, and he will show him even greater works than these, so that you will be amazed.'"**

That is why Jesus never failed. He was successful because He always knew God's will. He always knew where to go, what to do, how to do it, what to say, etc.

He knew He could heal the sick because He knew God empowered Him to do it (Luke 4:18-19). He knew God's will so He could not fall to temptation (Luke 4:12). He had God's mind so He had supernatural insight about people (John 1:42-51). His understanding and revelation of God's will made Him victorious.

## THE IMPORTANCE OF KNOWING GOD'S WILL

Knowing God's will is the difference between walking in victory or defeat. A previous friend of mine lived a very erratic, inconsistent life. One day he is called to be an evangelist so he moves his family to another state. A few months later he tells me he is called to be a pastor. A year or so later he is called to live in such and such state. A little while later he tells me that he has always been called to minister in a completely different state. This friend of mine has experienced very little to no forward movement in life because he has yet to discern God's will for him. He is trying, clearly, so I give him props, but he's experienced so much defeat because he does not know God's will.

Hosea 4:6 tells us, **"my people are destroyed from a lack of knowledge."** Likewise, Isaiah 5:13 says, **"Therefore my people will go into exile for a lack of understanding…"** You see, people are not defeated because the devil is big and bad. They are not defeated because their situation is abnormally difficult. They are defeated because there is something about God's will—who God is, what He will do, who He says we are and what He says we can do— that they are missing.

It is for this reason that the Apostle Paul writes in Ephesians 1:19 (NLT), **"I also pray that you will understand the incredible**

**greatness of God's power for us who believe him. This is the same mighty power that raised Christ from the dead and seated him in the place of honor at God's right hand in the heavenly realms."** Why would Paul take the time to pray for believers to realize the greatness of power we have through Christ even though it already belonged to us as believers? Because God's will for people, His promises, are not automatic. The mere existence of them does not mean they'll perform in our lives any more than the existence of soap means everyone is clean. They must be known and understood, and then believed and acted upon.

Think of it like this: Could one drive a car he did not know he owned? Of course not! In the same way, believers must know that they have received authority before they can exercise it. They must know it is God's will for them to be healed and walk in victory before they can believe God for it.

## WE CAN KNOW GOD'S WILL

What if I told you that you could walk in the same revelation and understanding of God's will as Jesus did, producing the same victory life He saw?

Most people have been taught to believe that's impossible. They say, "Don't you know that God's ways are higher than our ways and His thoughts higher than ours?" Or they'll say, "But that was Jesus." As we discussed in the previous chapter, Christ lives in us! A part of the way that manifests for us is in our minds. The Bible tells us that God has given us the *mind* of Christ!

1 Corinthians 2:15 (NLT) tells us:

"Those who are spiritual can evaluate all things, but they themselves cannot be evaluated by others. For,

'Who can know the Lord's thoughts?
Who knows enough to teach him?'

But we understand these things, FOR WE HAVE THE MIND OF CHRIST."

We have the mind of Christ so we can understand the thoughts of God—that's His will. We can think like Christ because as believers we have been given His mind.

So then the idea that God's will is so far beyond reach that we can't know it is unbiblical. Ephesians 5:17 tells us, **"Therefore do not be foolish, but understand what the Lord's will is."** We *can* know God's will. We are instructed to know it. The Bible goes as far as saying that to think otherwise is foolishness. After all, God wouldn't instruct us to do something we cannot do.

The question is: how do we think like Jesus and understand God's will like Jesus? In scripture, we can identify three ways how this happens:

**Understanding God's Will Through God's Word**

Jesus knew the Word of God. He studied it thoroughly. Even

from an early age Jesus was in the temple asking questions and learning about God's Word (Luke 2:41-49).

We can have Christ's understanding of God's will because we too can read and study the Word of God. We don't have to sit and wonder what is God's will is for our lives, we can turn to the Word. God's Word is His will. The Word is the standard for what we're to believe, think, have and do in life.

Additionally, the truths and covenant promises we read in the Bible are His will. For example, where Psalm 103:5 says, **"Praise the Lord, my soul, and forget not all his benefits—who forgives all your sins and heals all your diseases,"** we have a revelation of His will. We're not reading about a nice thing God will do when He feels like it. No! It *is* God's will to forgive. It *is* God's will to heal.

We must understand that since His Word *is* His will, that means God's truths and promises are His will for everyone—not just for some. If His Word is not His will for *me*, we have a huge problem on our hands. Allow me to explain:

The Bible says, **"For God so loved the world that he gave his one and only Son, that whoever believes in him shall not perish but have eternal life"** (John 3:16). Who can be saved? Whoever believes in Jesus. Whoever means anyone. If whoever did not mean anyone, how do you know it includes you? Perhaps whoever meant only 100 people—are you one of those 100? How do you go about finding out? Another scripture, maybe? Well, how are you supposed to know if that one doesn't include you, either?

You see, if God's will is His Word it must be His will for everyone because if it's not no one can know if it is for them. And if people don't know if it is God's will for them, they will doubt. And if they doubt, they do not and cannot have faith. Faith requires that we know it is God's will for *me*.

A victory life through Jesus Christ is for you because the promises are all-inclusive toward those who believe:

Healing includes you. James 5:14, **"Is anyone among you sick?"** Are you anyone?

Prosperity is for you. 2 Corinthians 8:9, **"For you know the grace of our Lord Jesus Christ, that though he was rich, yet for your sake he became poor, so that you through his poverty might become rich."** Or was only the Corinthian Church out of all the other churches and believers today permitted to prosper?

The gifts of the Holy Spirit are for you. 1 Corinthians 12:1-11, **"Now about the gifts of the Spirit, brothers and sisters…"** Are you a brother or sister in the faith?

The list goes on. God's Word is His will for you!

**Jesus' Life**

We can also understand God's will by looking at Jesus Himself. Hebrews 1:3 also says, **"the radiance of God's glory and the exact representation of his being."** This means that Jesus is the exact representation of who God is, what He desires and what He will do. Jesus said, **"For I have come down from heaven not to do my own will but to do the will of him who sent me"** (John 6:30).

Therefore, we can look at Jesus' earthly life—everything He did and did not do—to discover what is God's will. Whatever Jesus did, it was because it was God's will. And since we know we're supposed to be like Christ, that means it's God's will for us, too.

As we've discussed thus far, Jesus was a liberator. Jesus **"went around doing good and healing all who were under the power of the devil, because God was with him"** (Acts 10:38). So if liberating people was not God's will, Jesus spent His entire ministry violating it! But that's not the case. Rather, Jesus did good because God was with Him. It was God's will! Liberating people, then, is God's will for us.

Often times, people are convinced that Jesus does bad things to people to make them more spiritual. On one occasion a believer I was talking to said that God gave him cancer so he could develop more patience and trust. But we see in Acts 10:38 that Jesus was the one doing the good, the devil was the one doing the bad. In His earthly life, Jesus did not give a single person sickness. He did not make people blind, deaf or crippled. Such things were Satan's doings, even as Jesus Himself taught us (Luke 13:16, Matthew 12:22-28, Mark 9:14-29, Luke 4:40-41, etc.). These roles have not switched today: God's will is to do you good while Satan is the oppressor.

Moreover, Jesus did not turn a single person away for healing or deliverance. He never told them, "No." He healed them *all* because it was God's will to heal all.

Neither will Jesus turn away from healing or restoring your life! Hebrews 13:8 assures us this fact: **"Jesus Christ is the same yesterday and today and forever."**

**Revelation by the Spirit**

If the subject matter isn't specifically mentioned in the Word, we are not out of luck when it comes to knowing and understanding the Lord's will. Having Christ's mind also means having the ability to receive revelation about God's will for specific matters of our lives through the Holy Spirit who speaks to us and leads us in life.

Read 1 Corinthians 2:6-16.

The scripture says that God reveals what humans cannot understand or know to believers through the Holy Spirit: **"these are the things God has revealed to us by his Spirit."** This doesn't mean that God reveals extra-biblical doctrine to people. God's written Word is settled on doctrinal matters. What it means is that God wants to reveal to us meaning and application of the scriptures.

For example, we know that marriage is in God's will because of the Word. But through the Holy Spirit, God wants to lead us to *who* we should marry.

Or, for example, we know that having a job is in God's will. But where we should work and what we should do with our lives is specific direction we must receive from the Holy Spirit.

What does this look like? It is communion, conversation, between our spirit and God's Holy Spirit in us. As we pray with our understanding and in the Holy Spirit (Ephesians 6:18, 1 Corinthians 14:2), God will speak things to our spirit.

One way this manifests is that God will drop ideas or directions into our spirit. In Acts 27:10 Paul says, **"Men, I can see that our voyage is going to be disastrous and bring great loss to ship**

**and cargo, and to our own lives also."** Paul didn't figure this out because he was better at predicting weather and ocean conditions than sailors. No, it was a supernatural revelation Paul received by the Holy Spirit.

As the youth ministry where my wife and I were pastors started growing, we quickly realized we were going to need more leaders. So we gathered a team of leaders and began praying about how each person should be involved and serve. As we were praying, the idea came strongly across my mind that one of them really liked taking pictures—the professional camera kind, not the iPhone kind. After a few days of praying about it, I just couldn't dismiss the thought. So at our next leadership meeting I asked the individual: "Do you like taking pictures, like with an actual camera?" And they said, "I love to!" That person then became our core photographer for all of our youth events. It was because of that idea from the Holy Spirit that we were able to get the right person serving in the right place.

Another way the Holy Spirit speaks is a "feeling" of sorts in our spirit. Acts 16:6 says, **"Paul and his companions traveled throughout the region of Phrygia and Galatia, having been kept by the Holy Spirit from preaching the word in the province of Asia."** The Holy Spirit didn't come down in the form a block wall to prevent them from preaching in the province of Asia. It was simply a bad "feeling" Paul and his companions had preaching there, so they didn't go (see also: Acts 15:28).

If the thing we are praying about is God's will, it will be like a "green light" going off in our spirit. It will seem right. We will experience peace and joy (Isaiah 55:12).

But if the thing is not God's will, it will be like a "red light." Like Paul experienced, it will seem like a bad idea. You will have no joy or peace about it.

It is a plan of the devil to get believers to think they have to settle for ignorance, that there are "just some things we may never know," as many have supposed. Because if the devil can get us to believe that we can't know God's will in a situation, he'll stop us from going to the Lord in order to receive the revelation we need to walk in victory over his schemes. He'll stop us from having communion with the Holy Spirit.

## WHOLEHEARTED SEARCHING

If we are walking in uncertainty of His will and experiencing defeat in our lives, it is not because God is playing hide and seek. It is not because God wants to make it difficult for us to find Him. Nor is it because sometimes the answer is "yes" and other times it is "no." Matthew 7:7 says, **"Ask and it will be given to you; seek and you will find; knock and the door will be opened to you."** God will come to the door, He will open it, and we will be given our answer.

The hard truth of any uncertainty we face and defeat we experience is because we aren't actually searching Him out. Jeremiah 29:13-14 tells us, **"You will seek me and find me when you search for me with all of your heart. I will be found by you, declares the Lord…"**

It's like once when I went to look for some salsa in the

refrigerator. I opened the fridge, bent down, looked to the left and right but didn't immediately see it. So I called to my wife, "Alyssa, where's the salsa?"

She said, "In the fridge."

I responded, "I'm looking but I don't see it."

She got up, walked over to where I was beside the refrigerator, moved the milk and lo and behold there it was! It was there all along! It wasn't hiding. All I had to do was honestly, wholeheartedly look.

Too often people have a casual pursuit toward God. They casually arrive for church 10 minutes late. If their kids' extracurricular activities interfere with church, church is skipped to attend the event. They casually read their Bibles. They casually pray.

A casual heart toward God cannot find Him. God will either be everything or He will be nothing at all. He despises lukewarm Christian living (Revelation 3:16). He is actively looking for **"those whose hearts are fully committed to him"** to show Himself strong in them (2 Chronicles 16:9).

He wants our whole hearts. He has said we will find Him when we search for Him wholeheartedly. Be determined to find Him and you will.

*CHAPTER 3*

# FAITH TO BE AND DO

In order to be Jesus and do what Jesus did, we must have faith in the truths and promises of God that tell us we can. If we don't believe we can, we never will. For faith is what causes the miraculous to happen (Mark 9:23).

That is why having the mind of Christ—knowing God's will—as we discussed in the previous chapter is so crucial. If we don't even know God's promises, we certainly won't be able to have faith in them.

Over the years, I have had many believers tell me why they don't believe in divine healing or miracles. After I share scripture with them on the matter and talk about my own testimonies, they almost always ask something like, "If that's true, why am I not healed?" So I'll respond by saying, "Why are you surprised that you are not healed when you spent the last 20 minutes telling me how you don't believe in it? Could you expect to be saved if you didn't believe in salvation? Of course not!"

F.F. Bosworth writes, "Appropriating faith cannot go beyond

one's knowledge of the revealed will of God.²" We have to know God's will in order to have faith to see that thing come to pass. That's what Romans 10:17 (KJV) means in saying, **"So then faith cometh by hearing, and hearing by the word of God."**

Every one of the Lord's promises—from salvation to healing—are accessed by faith. Our entire "faith" works by faith:

**"For we live by faith, not by sight."**

2 Corinthians 5:7

**"And my righteous ones will live by faith. But I will take no pleasure in anyone who turns away."**

Hebrews 10:38 NLT

**"This Good News tells us how God makes us right in his sight. This is accomplished from start to finish by faith…"**

Romans 1:17 NLT

**"He said to her, 'Daughter, your faith has healed you. Go in peace and be freed from your suffering.'"**

Mark 5:34

God is a faith God. He requires all who come to Him to have faith. Without faith, **"it is impossible to please God, because anyone who comes to him must believe that he exists and that he rewards those who earnestly seek him"** (Hebrews 11:6). If we don't believe, we doubt and cannot receive Him or any of His promises.

## DEFINING FAITH

Hebrews 11:1 defines faith. It says, **"Now faith is confidence in what we hope for and assurance about what we do not see."** There are two parts to this scripture, thus, two parts to the definition of faith: First, faith is confidence in what we hope for; second, faith is assurance about what we don't see.

**Faith is Confidence**

First, faith is confidence. It is not hope. Hope lacks confidence. Hope isn't sure what will happen. It hopes for an outcome, but isn't sure it will happen. It just "hopes." Faith, however, is *confident* hope: **"Now faith is confidence in what we hope for…"**

Hope says, quite literally, "I hope…" Faith says, "I know…" Think about this in terms of salvation. When we believe in Christ's forgiveness, we don't say, "I hope I'm saved" but "I know I am saved." This is because faith is complete confidence in God to do what He said He will do. The NLT translation reads, **"Faith is the confidence that what we hope for will actually happen…"** This is where most people get stuck in terms of faith. They believe God *can* but question if He *will*.

In Mark 5, we read of a woman who suffered from bleeding for 12 years. When Jesus came to town, she said to herself, **"If I just touch his clothes, I will be healed"** (Mark 5:27). So she pushed through the crowd around Him, touched Him and was instantly healed. A few verse later Jesus says to her, **"Daughter, your faith has healed you"** (Mark 5:34). He called her confidence "faith." She did not say, "I hope I will be healed." She said, "I *will* be."

It was by this confident faith, according to Jesus, that she was healed. It was not "if it's God's will" she would be healed or "in God's timing" she would be healed. Jesus didn't pull her aside, sit her down and say, "Listen, you can't approach God like that. Who do you think you are being so pushy, telling *God* to heal you?" No! It was already God's will and it was already His timing. It took her having confidence in Jesus—faith—to obtain it. She didn't touch Him in hope, she touched Him with purpose, in expectation, in confidence, in faith. She believed Jesus could *and would* as she reached out in faith to touch Him.

James 1:6-8 tells us:

**"But when you ask, you must believe and not doubt, because the one who doubts is like a wave of the sea, blown and tossed by the wind. That person should not expect to receive anything from the Lord. Such a person is double-minded and unstable in all they do."**

Doubt is not faith because it has no idea what God will or will not do. Doubt is uncertainty. When people pray like this, "God, if it's your will, heal me. But if it's not, just give me strength" it reveals they have no idea what God will or will not do. They are uncertain. They have doubt. As the above scripture in James explains, they are double-minded. They go back and forth on what God's will is for them. They believe He can, but question if He will. They believe He exists, but they are uncertain that He rewards—they go back and forth on God's will. This matters because James goes on to say the person who doubts, **"should not expect to receive anything from the Lord."** Doubting ensures we receive nothing from God, not salvation, not an answer to prayer, not healing, not direction in life, not prosperity, nothing. Why? Because faith is how God works. God is a faith God. Without faith in Him—that He exists *and* that He is a rewarder, a do-gooder of men—it is impossible to please Him.

In today's generation, the idea of someone doubting or having a lack of faith is nothing short of an insult. I have had numerous people sneer at me, asking, "Are you saying I have a lack of faith?!" The unfortunate answer for their pride's sake is: possibly, yes. If *Jesus* stated that people's lack of faith was the cause of a lack of victory or healing (Matthew 17:20, Matthew 21:21, Matthew 8:26, etc.), then surely having a lack of faith today is a real possibility.

We must also realize that doubting will cause us to fall short as liberators for others. On one occasion, the disciples were unable to cast an evil spirit out of a young boy. When they asked Jesus why they were unable, He said, **"Because of your unbelief"** (Matthew 17:20 KJV). They lacked faith, they doubted. Perhaps they weren't sure if it was God's will to heal the boy. Perhaps they weren't sure if they had the power to cast out devil as Jesus had told them. Either way, doubting and uncertainty left them, and will leave us today, as "wonderers" absent of any and all power to do anything about others' situations.

Let us therefore maintain full confidence in God. Hebrews 10:35, **"So do not throw away your confidence; it will be richly rewarded."** Our faith working as confidence in God's Word will see to it that we walk in victory and stand as a liberators!

### Faith is Assurance Despite Sight

Second, faith is **"assurance about what we do not see."** It believes God's Word above anything perceived in the sense realm. The opposite of faith isn't doubt, the opposite of faith is sight. This is what the Bible means when it says, **"we walk by faith not by sight" (2 Corinthians 5:17 KJV).**

Concerning Jesus' resurrection, Thomas said, **"Unless I see the nail marks in his hands and put my finger where the nails were, and put my hand into his side, I will not believe"** (John 20:25). He refused to believe Jesus had risen from the dead until he could see Jesus himself and feel his scars. His belief was based on sense knowledge—what he could see, hear, feel, touch and rationalize.

Jesus appeared to Thomas about a week later, Jesus rebuked him, saying, **"Because you have seen me, you have believed; blessed are those who have not seen and yet have believed"** (John 20:29). Jesus explained that true faith is not based on what one can perceive. Rather, it is based on what one believes from the Word of God—for Jesus had previously told them He would rise from the dead (Matthew 16:21). They needed to believe His Words, not just believe once He was risen. So then, faith believes God's Word over any natural fact, evidence, measurable substance or rational.

Belief that is based on sight or sense knowledge says:

"I don't have the money."

"I'm sick."

"I don't have the ability."

It says something that takes zero faith to say—something natural, not supernatural. For it doesn't take any faith to say something which one already sees. No, faith sees what the sense knowledge cannot see.

Even after having just read one of God's promises, those who are dominated by the sense realm will remain absent of faith. They'll say, "I know the Bible says God heals, but my back is still hurting so maybe it's not His will for me to be healed."

But being "in faith" means us saying, "I'm going to believe the Word *over* what I can see and feel." Faith is when the truthfulness of God's promises far outweighs what we can perceive in the natural realm. It's deciding to believe and hold on to God's promises as true even if they have yet to occur in the natural realm.

This was how Abraham, the great patriarch of our faith, lived and believed:

**"Without weakening in his faith, he faced the fact that his body was as good as dead--since he was about a hundred years old--and that Sarah's womb was also dead. Yet he did not waver through unbelief regarding the promise of God, but was strengthened in his faith and gave glory to God, being fully persuaded that God had power to do what he had promised."**

Romans 4:19-21

It doesn't make any sense to say, "I'm 100 years old, of course I will have a child." Yet Abraham disregarded "fact" for the Word of God.

Therefore, to have faith for healing, for example, it makes more sense to say, "I am healed" rather than "I am sick." One does not need evidence from doctors or a certain feeling to know if the Bible is true. One simply regards God's Word as the ultimate truth and everything else a lie. As the Bible says, **"Let God be true, and every human being a liar** (Romans 3:4).

## FAITH IS FOR THE NOW

Since faith is complete confidence in God's promises despite the natural senses, faith is for the "now." That is, faith makes us a possessor of what God has promised in order to change present condition.

Hope always pushes the fulfillment of God's promises out into the future. For instance, people will say, "I believe I will be healed *one day*." Faith, however, says, "It is done."

Faith working in this manner is how all of God's promises are meant to operate. Consider how salvation works. When we confess faith in Christ, we become a possessor of salvation. The Bible says, **"…and with the mouth one confesses and is saved"** (Romans 10:10 KJV). We don't say, "I know I'll be saved one day." No, we say, "I believe therefore I *am* saved."

In another example, the Bible goes as far as saying that we *are* citizens of heaven—even though we live on earth (Philippians 3:20). Faith makes us a possessor of heaven before we ever get there.

Jesus himself operated in this manner. Notice how Jesus responded when Jairus' daughter died in Luke 8:52-55:

**"Meanwhile, all the people were wailing and mourning for her. 'Stop wailing,' Jesus said. 'She is not dead but asleep.' They laughed at him, knowing that she was dead. But he took her by the hand and said, 'My child, get up!' Her spirit returned, and at once she stood up. Then Jesus told them to give her something to eat."**

Jesus wasn't out of his mind by saying she was only sleeping. Nor was everyone just mistaken about her being dead. No, the girl was actually dead. Jesus was simply speaking in faith. He called her resurrection done before it actually was so.

Jesus instructs us to operate in faith in that same manner. Pertaining to all matters of faith and victory, Jesus said in Mark 11:24, **"Therefore I tell you, whatever you ask for in prayer, believe that you have received it, and it will be yours."** We are to believe we *have* received it, not that we will receive it. We are to consider it done the moment we pray. It is believing we *have* received it that ensures we will actually receive it.

Similarly, 1 John 5:14-15 states: **"This is the confidence we have in approaching God: that if we ask anything according to his will, he hears us. And if we know that he hears us— whatever we ask—WE KNOW THAT WE HAVE what we**

**asked of him."** Yet again, we are to consider that we have it the moment we ask. God doesn't just hear us, He grants it to us when we ask.

So let us stop praying in hope: "One day I know I'll be healed." No! We are people of faith. We are possessors of what God has promised because we believe. We say instead, "I believe God has heard me and that it is mine."

Start praising God now that what you've been praying for is done. For your faith has made you a possessor of what God has promised!

## HOW TO GET FAITH

At their own confession, many believers struggle to get faith. They say, "I can't seem to get faith." They act as if faith is running from them and is something that must be caught.

But the Bible says that faith will *come*. You don't have to chase it, it will come to you. The Bible says, **"Faith COMETH by hearing, and hearing by the word of God"** (Romans 10:17 KJV). How do you make faith come to you? It said "by the Word of God." You make faith come to you by going to the Word. By reading and understanding the Word of God, faith will come to us.

The Bible says that the Word of God is like a seed (Luke 8:11). When a seed is properly planted and received by the soil, it will produce a crop. But if no crops are being produced, we don't question if the seed is good. We don't try to get a refund on the seeds. No, we know that the problem is how the seed was *received* by the soil. The same is true concerning the Word of God. If the covenant promises and victory in the Bible aren't happening in our lives, the problem isn't the Word of God, the problem is how it's been *received*.

The Word of God is properly received only by our hearts. Our hearts are the soil to the Word of God. David said, **"I have hidden your word in my heart that I might not sin against you"** (Psalm 119:11). After the Israelite spies returned from spying out the land of Canaan, Caleb said, **"I brought him word again as it was in mine heart."** (Joshua 14:7 KJV).

A head knowledge of what God has said can't generate faith and produce God's promises. Having a head knowledge is memorizing the Word or even agreeing with the Word that it's good and true, but it doesn't actually believe it. Only when the Word takes root in our hearts will we have faith and see God's promises come about.

We know what's in our hearts by how we speak. The Bible says, **"For the mouth speaks what the heart is full of"** (Luke 6:45). So when the Word isn't in our hearts—that is, it's just something we've memorized—we'll start speaking the opposite of what the Word says. At church we'll say, "Praise God! Healing is for me." But then at home or work, we'll say things like, "I know I'll be the first one to get sick this flu season." We're speaking what's actually in our hearts, which isn't the Word.

On the other hand, you'll know when the Word has taken root in your heart when not even someone *else* can speak contrary to the Word of God about you and you get uncomfortable. You'll say to yourself, "That's not me! That's not my story!"

We'll never be able to get God's Word to take root in our hearts and get faith if we have surrounded ourselves with doubters and mockers. Before Jesus raised Jairus' daughter from the dead, He sent the mourners, those who did not believe Jesus could heal the girl, out of the house (Mark 5:21-43). He separated Himself from the influence of doubters.

Doubters speak negativity, sickness and fear into themselves and others. They mock our confidence in God saying how we "just got lucky last time" or how we're "taking this whole faith thing too far." We can't expect to have pure faith when we've allowed doubters to speak into our ears just as much as we have allowed the Word to speak to us. We can't expect to have pure faith when we attend a church that doesn't believe in healing, prosperity or victory.

Whether it be our friends or family members who are doubters and mockers, we must draw a line of separation so we're not influenced into doubting. And if the voice of doubt and mocking is coming from our church, we should find a full gospel church immediately. We still love mockers and doubters, of course, but we must refuse to allow doubt to be spoken into our spirits if we want be strong in faith so we can walk as liberators and in victory in life.

## ALL THINGS POSSIBLE

Jesus said, **"Everything is possible for one who believes"** (Mark 9:23). Faith makes all things possible. The impossible happening is not up to God. God is the God of the impossible, but Jesus pinned it on us to put faith to work and cause the fulfillment of God's promises.

Ephesians 3:20 also tells us, **"Now to him who is able to do immeasurably more than all we ask or imagine, according to his power that is at work within us."** His power is at work within us. It's stored, waiting to be released.

This is much like what we learned in science class about potential energy. Potential energy is an object's stored energy because of its position. For example, a wrecking ball that has been pulled back, ready to swing, has tremendous energy *available*. Yet it is only when the ball is released—that it's put into motion—that such power is utilized.

Likewise, when we position ourselves in faith, we are in a position of power where all things become possible. When we've taken the time to build ourselves up in the Word and *know* the Lord, we won't look at the impossible situation as if it's an impossible situation. For we'll know "everything is possible." We know the power *available*.

But "is possible" is a contingency. Believing makes it possible, but it's not until such faith is *put into motion* that the immeasurably great power of the Lord takes effect. Hebrews 11:30 says, **"By faith the walls of Jericho fell, AFTER the army had marched around them for seven days."** It was after they moved. They had faith in God's promise that the walls would fall, but they needed to get in motion for it to take effect. Belief that isn't put into motion is powerless.

This is what Jesus explains in Luke 6:46-49. He says that it's the one who hears His Words *and* puts them to practice that stands firm; whereas the one who hears His Words and does not put them to practice will collapse and be destroyed.

How we release our faith and put it to motion is by our words (speaking) and actions. Doing so causes the ball of faith, if you will, to swing, destroying the work of the enemy and ushering in God's promises.

**Faith Speaks**

Since faith has complete confidence in the Lord even despite what it can see, faith speaks. 2 Corinthians 4:13: **"It is written: 'I believed; therefore I have spoken.' Since we have that same spirit of faith, we also believe and therefore speak."** Faith speaks out God's promises because it believes God's promises to be true. It speaks victory because it believes God promises victory. It speaks righteousness because it believes in the sacrifice of Jesus Christ. Faith says:

"Because God says so, He is."

"Because God says so, He will."

"Because God says so, I am."

"Because God says so, I have."

"Because God says so, I am able."

Faith boldly speaks out God's Word because it knows His Word must come to pass, that it must perform in our lives.

In Hebrews 10:23, we are adjured to **"hold unswervingly to the hope we profess, for he who promised is faithful."** To hold unswervingly means to not say one thing and then in the next breath say the opposite. It means to be consistent in speaking out the promises of God. The KJV translates it as, **"hold fast the profession of our faith"**—to hold tightly, firmly, to what we believe.

There is a problem with our speaking if how we talk about God, His goodness and His promises changes based on the situation we are in. One will find that people are so quick to change from, "God, you're so good and faithful!" on Sunday morning to, "Where are you, God? Why have you abandoned me?" come Monday evening. They say, "God is my healer," but when the doctor's report comes they say, "Well, maybe it's not His will to heal me." They do not hold firmly to His promise.

How we speak is important because from God's Word we can clearly see that what we say matters—why we're instructed to hold fast to what we believe! Over and over again we see that our words have power:

**"From the fruit of their mouth a person's stomach is filled; with the harvest of their lips they are satisfied. The tongue has the power of life and death, and those who love it will eat its fruit."**

Proverbs 18:20-21

**"Those who guard their lips preserve their lives, but those who speak rashly will come to ruin."**

Proverbs 13:3

**"Those who guard their mouths and their tongues keep themselves from calamity."**

Proverbs 20:23

Recall how our words play a vital role in our salvation. It is by our believing that we are made righteous and by the words of our mouth that we are saved. As Romans 10:9-10 says:

**"That if thou shalt confess with thy mouth the Lord Jesus, and shalt believe in thine heart that God hath raised him from the dead, thou shalt be saved. For with the heart man believeth unto righteousness; and with the mouth confession is made unto salvation."**

Since our words are important enough to be involved in the process of salvation, we're not being hyper-spiritual or out of our minds by saying our words have power. We are being scriptural. What we say carries power. By our words we bring into manifestation God's promises.

Jesus said in Mark 11:23 (KJV), **"For verily I say unto you, That whosoever shall SAY unto this mountain, Be thou removed, and be thou cast into the sea; and shall not doubt in his heart, but shall believe that those things which he saith shall come to pass; he shall have whatsoever he saith."** Jesus has given us authority and power to speak to the mountains, any work of the enemy in our lives, and command them to be uprooted.

So in circumstantial moments, we don't want to remain silent but speak out God's promise. If there's a mountain of sickness or poverty in your life, tell it to move in Jesus' name. And certainly don't change your confession to one of defeat.

One of the best ways to be proactively confess and declare the Word over our lives in faith is to develop a daily confession. Every morning when I wake up, there are a host of scriptural confessions that I declare over my life. To name a few:

- I have self-control. Christ in me is stronger than any wrong desire against me.
- I don't get sick, I heal the sick.
- I have an abundance of finances and am a giver.
- I am anointed and more than able to conquer any challenge set before me.

What one will discover is that as he begins confessing the Word, holding to it regardless the situation, even if he doesn't quite believe it completely he is building faith and destroying doubt in himself. How? Because **"faith cometh by hearing, and hearing by the word of God."** He is forcing himself with his own mouth to hear and get the Word in his heart.

As a guard over what we believe and speak, I challenge you to say out loud, "And that's just the way I like it" after *everything* you say. Doing so draws our attention to what we're saying so we can check to see if it lines up with the Word of God.

**Faith Acts**

Similarly to speaking, faith acts.

In Luke 5, Jesus instructed Simon to get back into his boat to go out to catch some fish. Simon responded by saying, **"Master, we've worked hard all night and haven't caught anything. But because you say so, I will let down the nets"** (Luke 5:5). The KJV renders it, **"nevertheless at thy word I will."** Simon was willing to act and obey Jesus' words regardless of what he could perceive or understand.

Faith puts God's Word to work by action. It considers God's Word to be true so it simply does what God's Word says to do. It doesn't pay attention to what can be perceived in the natural.

The Bible tells us, **"In the same way, faith by itself, if it is not accompanied by action, is dead"** (James 2:17). If we can't act on what God has said, then it indicates to us that there is a faith problem. We would need to get our eyes on the Word instead of the facts of our circumstances.

Acting on our faith is important because without action we cannot reap the promise of God we are believing for. If Simon had not gone back out to fish, it would not have mattered what Jesus' said (His Word), Simon would have caught absolutely zero fish. Likewise, James tells us about Abraham:

**You foolish person, do you want evidence that faith without deeds is useless? Was not our father Abraham considered righteous for what he did when he offered his son Isaac on the altar? You see that his faith and his actions were working together, and his faith was made complete by what he did. And the scripture was fulfilled that says, "Abraham believed God,**

**and it was credited to him as righteousness," and he was called God's friend. You see that a person is considered righteous by what they do and not by faith alone.**

James 2:20-24

Our actions and our faith work together. What we do is vital. It is not blaspheming to emphasize works—our works and faith go hand in hand. And if what we physically do is necessary for something as important as faith for *righteousness*, as the scripture above states in the case with Abraham, how important also are our actions with God's other promises!

Therefore, faith is not waiting for God's promises to be fulfilled. It is not hoping for them to happen one day in the future. Faith is taking the required action prescribed in God's Word to enforce their fulfillment.

Hebrews 11:33-35 says:

**"who through faith conquered kingdoms, administered justice, and gained what was promised; who shut the mouths of lions, quenched the fury of the flames, and escaped the edge of the sword; whose weakness was turned to strength; and who became powerful in battle and routed foreign armies. Women received back their dead, raised to life again…"**

They weren't waiting in hope. They didn't say, "One day I know I'll gain victory over this army." Their faith was in the "now." It was them putting God's Word to work to cause what God had promised to come to pass. For instance, as Caleb said after God promised that the land of Canaan (the Promised Land) belonged to the Israelites: **"We should go up and take possession of the land, for we can certainly do it"** (Numbers 13:30). Their faith was in the "now" so it required action. If their faith was hope, thinking it will happen "one day," they never would've taken it even though God promised it.

My wife and I learned this first hand after our first daughter was born. Soon after birth she had developed some blood complications that turned serious very quickly. My wife and I prayed, others prayed, pastors prayed, yet our daughter only grew worse.

Upon being told that we needed to transfer to another hospital due to the seriousness of our daughter's complications, we reached a breaking point. Full of faith, my wife looked at me and said, "Josiah, this is our baby and this sickness cannot happen." And so we agreed that we would simply believe her healing was done, that God had healed her. My wife proceeded to take her out of the BiliBed which she was being kept in, and she called the nurse to test her again, that God had healed her.

Of course, the doctors explained to us that testing her again was pointless because they had just tested her. They said, "We believe in God, too, but it just doesn't work that way." They also told us that we needed to put her back in the BiliBed. But my wife just smiled and said, "No, God has healed her. Test her again."

An hour later we got the test results and everything was normal! The nurses and doctors were stunned. They ordered three more tests and all came back normal! At one point, they even checked our daughter's identity tag because they were under the suspicion that we had stolen someone else's baby!

If we would have only continued praying and "believing," our daughter may have developed cereal palsy. Without action working with our faith, our faith was dead. It was when action was joined with our faith that we saw God's promise to heal manifest.

## STAND FIRM

I see you moving mountains and liberating the captives in Jesus' name! **"Stand firm in the faith"** (1 Corinthians 16:13 NLT). Speak God's promises in boldness. Take action on His Word. Put God's power to work—don't be idle! The impossible ends for you today!

*CHAPTER 4*

# LIVING RIGHTEOUSLY

The Bible tells us in 1 Peter 2:24, **"He himself bore our sins in his body on the cross, so that we might die to sins and live for righteousness…"** God's will in sending Jesus to die for our sins was so that we would live for righteousness. That is, God wanted to give us power to live righteously just like Jesus had power to live righteously. Jesus' level of righteousness isn't to be something we marvel at, it's something we are to replicate.

## RIGHTEOUS LIVING IS POSSIBLE

There have been many churches and religious leaders to say that righteous living isn't really possible. They say things like, "You're going to sin, you're going to make mistakes," or "We all sin every day." They magnify the power of sin so much so that sinful Christian living is thought to be normal. One popular song's lyrics read: "I've been a sinner, I've been a saint, a little bit a both every single day."

Accepting sin as normal is not how God has called us to live. He has called us to live in complete victory over sin. That is how Jesus lived. He did not "have His issues." He was tempted in every way and did not sin a single time.

Remember, Jesus is not just a figure to marvel at. We are to be like Him in every way. 1 John 2:6 says, **"Whoever claims to live in him must live as Jesus did."** That certainly includes living sin free.

The following truths reveal why we never have to be sinful, that we have received power to live righteously:

**Jesus Bore Our Sinfulness**

1 Peter 2:24 said that Jesus, **"bore our sins"** on the cross. Bore means that Jesus took our sins on Himself. He received them as His own even though He was sinless and took the punishment for them. Isaiah 53:5 says, **"But he was pierced for our transgressions, he was crushed for our iniquities; the punishment that brought us peace was on him."**

Jesus bore not merely our sinful deeds, He bore our sinful nature. Romans 6:6 says, **"For we know that our old self was crucified with him so that the body ruled by sin might be done away with, that we should no longer be slaves to sin."** And as Paul said about himself, **"I have been crucified with Christ and I no longer live, but Christ lives in me…"** (Galatians 2:20). When Jesus died, He died in our place. He was the stand-in for us. It was you and I nailed to the cross through His being nailed to the cross. Our old, sinful self was crucified with Him.

Therefore, since Jesus bore our sin there is no reason for us to bear it. If we have to be sinful, Jesus didn't do His job because He was supposed to bear it. But since He did in fact bear our sinful nature, there is no reason or excuse to be sinful.

We are not "sinners saved by grace," we *were* sinners who have been saved by grace. 1 Corinthians 6:11, **"And that is what some of you WERE. But you were washed…"** To say otherwise would be to say that Jesus has cleansed us from sin, yet we are still dirty with sin. It can only be one or the other!

What about what Paul said: **"of whom I am the worst"** (1 Timothy 1:15)? We need to read the preceding verses: **"Even though I was ONCE a blasphemer and a persecutor and a violent man, I was shown mercy…"** (1 Timothy 1:13). Paul *was* those things. He was speaking about his past, when he used to be "Saul." But he was changed by the blood of Jesus and received a new name: Paul. That new name signified the newness of life he found in Christ. His old self had died, Jesus bore it, so he never had to be that person again.

**Christ in You**

As we discussed in the first chapter of this book, once we accept Christ, He comes and lives in us. Colossians 1:27 (NLT) says, **"Christ lives in you."**

After our old self dies with Christ on the cross, we don't get a new life like in a video game—a re-try at life to do better. No, we receive Christ's life. Paul said in Galatians 2:20 (NLT), **"My old self has been crucified with Christ. It is no longer I who live, but**

**Christ lives in me…"** We have the right to say the same thing as Paul. We no longer live. But yet we're alive? Yes, that's Christ in us. We have received a new life that is in Him.

To say that we have to be sinful would say that Christ who lives in us is weaker than the sin that's in the world. God forbid! Jesus who is in us is stronger than any temptation against us (1 John 4:4).

### God's Mercy in Temptation

As an added bonus to the grace of sending His Son into the world, God continues to be merciful to us when it comes to temptation. The Bible tells us in 1 Corinthians 10:13, **"And God is faithful; he will not let you be tempted beyond what you can bear. But when you are tempted, he will also provide a way out so that you can endure it."** There are two powerful truths we can pull from this:

First, God won't allow us to be tempted beyond what we can bear. He doesn't just let *any* temptation come our way. If He doesn't think we can conquer the temptation, He won't allow it to come near us. How merciful! And if He has allowed it to tempt us, He knows we can beat it.

People say, "I just can't stop." If you're a believer, you can. To say otherwise calls God a liar. It would be saying not only that Jesus' sacrifice was insufficient, but also that God allowed you to be tempted with something you could not bear.

Second, God always provides a way of escape from the temptation. He not only protects us from the temptations we cannot overcome, He even provides a way out of the ones that He knows we *can*! Praise God! We need only to go through the door of escape He has opened for us.

## IMPORTANCE OF RIGHTEOUS LIVING

In order to do the same things Jesus did and greater (John 14:12), we must live the life He lived. The Bible tells us, **"Students are not greater than their teacher, and slaves are not greater than their master"** (Matthew 10:24 NLT).

We can't expect to produce the same level of miracles and healings as Jesus if we aren't willing and obedient to consecrate ourselves to the same level of righteousness. This is probably the biggest "how" in being like Jesus that we spoke about in the introduction of the book. We can't excuse sin simply because we're under grace. If we want to be liberators we must live righteously.

All too often, however, righteous living is excused and pushed to the backburner in the name of grace. People say, "We all sin every day." I call this being hyper-grace. It makes our "works" inconsequential.

While we are justified by grace through faith and not by works (Ephesians 2:8), it's not as if what we do once we confess faith in Christ no longer matters. Once we are saved, we have an obligation to live righteously. Romans 8:12-13 tells us:

**"Therefore, brothers and sisters, we have an obligation—but it is not to the flesh, to live according to it. For if you live**

**according to the flesh, you will die; but if by the Spirit you put to death the misdeeds of the body, you will live."**

Notice that this was written to believers, not unbelievers. Or how could an unbeliever live by the Spirit? No, we who believe must by the Spirit put to death the misdeeds of the flesh.

This is why when Jesus Himself spoke to the churches in the Book of Revelation, he said, **"I know your deeds…"** (Revelation 3:1, Revelation 3:8, Revelation 3:15). He didn't say, "You know, I see what you're doing and how your living but don't worry about it, my blood's got your back." No! He instructed them to stop what they were *doing* and *do* righteous things.

We must understand that we are not *earning* salvation or the favor of God on our lives by living righteously. Christ leveled the playing field in that aspect. We were all sinners when He died for us (Romans 5:8), so none of us could earn it or boast in ourselves. Rather, we are responsible for continuing in the grace poured out to us so that we don't fall away but instead access more of His grace for victory over sin (1 Peter 5:6, James 4:6). Colossians 1:22-23 tells us:

**"But now he has reconciled you by Christ's physical body through death to present you holy in his sight, without blemish and free from accusation—IF YOU CONTINUE in your faith, established and firm, and do not move from the hope held out in the gospel."**

We have received power to overcome sin and we are expected to use that power to put sin to death in our lives every day. What we do with the grace of God on our lives after salvation is our complete responsibility. That's what the Bible means when it says, **"For God is working in you, giving you the desire and the power to do what pleases him"** (Philippians 2:13). God isn't forcing any believer to be righteous. He is continually issuing us the grace we need to live victoriously, grace which we must put to work.

**Becoming a Special Utensil**

Varying levels of obedience to this sanctifying work of the Holy Spirit at work in us is why believers are at different levels in life. Some believers are struggling to overcome addiction and put sin to death. Others have completely fallen away from God (2 Peter 3:14-17, Galatians 5:4). Then there are those who are winning souls and being used to perform miracles and heal the sick. The reason for the disparity is not that God loves the latter more, but that they have stood more firm against sin, taken the time to consecrate themselves in prayer and fasting and have been more dedicated in reading the Word. The latter received the same desire and power (Philippians 2:13) as the other believers, but they responded to it at a higher level of consecration and obedience so it yielded higher results. They did not earn God's blessings, they accessed his blessing by living righteously.

This is the problem with the hyper-grace mentality. It creates an environment of sin comfortableness that enables people to fall away instead of provoking them to be holy like Christ. For example, I have seen several churches with the phrase "No Perfect People Allowed" as one of their core values. This doesn't provoke holiness, it permits sin. I would argue that it even makes perfection out to be a bad thing. Clearly, sin is the problem, not holiness. Sin is the destroyer of lives, families and destinies. In no way, shape, or form should we be advocating for unholiness.

The Bible tells us that once we are saved we *are* perfect before God. Romans 8:1 says, **"Therefore, there is now no condemnation for those who are in Christ Jesus."** No condemnation means perfection before God. It means God is holding nothing against us. So what we should be saying is "Perfect People Are Created Here."

For this reason Paul told Timothy, **"If you keep yourself pure, you will be a special utensil for honorable use. Your life will be clean, and you will be ready for the Master to use you for every good work."** (2 Timothy 2:21 NLT). According to Paul's analogy, a believer who allows sin into his life makes himself to be like a dirty fork that needs washed again. He isn't ready to be used when the dinner table is set, another utensil has to be used.

God wants us to be ready to be used by Him—that's why He sent Jesus to forgive us and make us righteous in the first place! But if we keep allowing sin into our lives, we force God's priorities to shift from "needing to use him" to "needing to work on his holiness."

Samson is a prominent Biblical example of this. He was called to be used by God to deliver the Israelites as a judge, so he was to take the vow of a Nazirite (Judges 13, Numbers 6)—a group of Israelites who took a vow of special consecration before the Lord. Because of this consecration, the Spirit of the Lord was able to come on Samson, making him extremely strong.

For years, Samson was used by God to deliver—to liberate—the Israelites from Philistine oppression. But over time, little by little, he developed a lax attitude toward consecration and sin. And eventually the Spirit of God left him (Judges 16:20). Consecration ensured he could be used mightily, but sinful living stole that from him.

In the same way, Spirit-filled believers who consecrate themselves to the Lord in righteousness make themselves available to be used mightily by God as liberators. They become special utensils for God to use. They will do the same things Jesus did, and greater (John 14:12). They will see dynamic answers to prayer: **"The prayer of a righteous person is powerful and effective"** (James 5:26).

Decide today that you will be one of those who go higher in God. Humble yourself by consecrating yourself to a level of righteousness where others aren't willing to go to, and you'll receive grace to go higher than they go (James 4:6).

**Having and Increasing in Boldness**

Being bold means being brave or having an absence of fear. The Bible tells us that fear is a spirit not of God (2 Timothy 1:7). That means it is a demonic spirit. It will bind us in anxiety, prevent us from walking in God's plan for our lives, prevent us from being liberators and prevent us from praying in confidence so we obtain the promises of God. The only way to overcome fear is to walk in the boldness that comes through being in Christ.

Ephesians 3:12 (KJV) says, **"In whom we have boldness…"** The "whom" here is Jesus. When we are in Christ we find boldness. How? Because of our identity: we are perfect before God (Romans 8:1, 1 Corinthians 1:30, 2 Corinthians 5:21). We are new creations. He holds nothing against us. In other words, He is on our side. And **"If God is for us, who can be against us?"** (Romans 8:31). That is why Proverbs 28:1 deems those who are righteous **"bold as a lion."** We turn from nothing, like a lion, because God is with us and for us. We will boldly pray, boldly heal the sick, boldly preach the gospel—we'll turn from nothing.

It takes continuing in righteous living to make that boldness grow. 1 John 3:21-22 tells us, **"Dear friends, if our hearts do not condemn us, we have confidence before God and receive from him anything we ask, BECAUSE WE KEEP HIS COMMANDS AND DO WHAT PLEASES HIM."** This means boldness grows when we're pressing forward in righteous living, not when we're constantly repenting.

By having to constantly repent we keep ourselves fighting against condemnation, which steals our confidence before God. Pressing forward in righteousness is the purpose of the new creation. It's not so we can repent but so that we can stop sinning (1 John 2:1).

I believe this is also why the devil has tried so hard to worm his way into the church with doctrines that tell Christians, "We all sin every day. We're just sinners saved by grace." Because if he can get believers to become sin conscious and battling sin he will zap their boldness. As E.W. Kenyon writes, "Sin makes cowards of men. Sin consciousness holds us in bondage.[3]"

The Bible tells us that the work of Christ was meant to **"cleanse our consciences"** (Hebrews 9:14). Telling the righteous they are still sinners is not a cleansing of conscience, it's fear inducing condemnation that prevents people from coming **"boldly to the throne of grace"** (Hebrews 4:16). It makers beggars out of the saints. And begging is not faith. Begging will not get God's promises to come to pass.

Make a commitment and plan to press forward in righteousness so boldness will grow in your spirit. 1 Corinthians 9:24-27 (NLT) says, **"So I run with purpose in every step. I am not just shadowboxing. I discipline my body like an athlete, training it to do what it should do…"** A boxer that doesn't make a training plan but just says, "I'll win when I get in the ring" will die. He has to make a plan. He must do everything with purpose—from what he eats, to how he trains, to when he sleeps.

Righteousness works the same way. If the only time we think about living righteously is when we're in the middle of a temptation, we will get beat up every time. We have to make a plan to move forward—get better and stronger—in righteousness.

Make a plan. When are you going to pray? When are you going to read the Word? What books by anointed men and women of God are you going to read this year? What are some weak spots in your righteousness or faith that you specifically need to work on?

As you carry out your righteousness plans, boldness will grow in your spirit just like it does for the athlete who trains faithfully. He knows he's getting stronger and better so the fear of the fight leaves his spirit and is replaced with boldness and tenacity.

## PUT ON THE NEW MAN

Ephesians 4:24 (NLT) tells us, **"Put on your new nature, created to be like God--truly righteous and holy."** This means realizing who Christ made you to be and living that way. Ultimately, we have to stop thinking that we are just "sinners saved by grace" if we want to succeed in righteous living.

The Bible says, **"For as he thinketh in his heart, so is he"** (Proverbs 23:7 KJV). If all we've done is talk defeat, can we honestly be surprised when we get defeated? Of course not. If we've spent all day confessing, "I know in the future I'm going to screw up again," we give that very sin permission and strength over us! We think and say out loud that it's stronger than Christ in us, so that's exactly what happens. The battle is all in the mind, in our perception of the work of Christ in us.

This is why the Apostle Paul instructs us:

**In the same way, count yourselves dead to sin but alive to God in Christ Jesus. Therefore do not let sin reign in your mortal body so that you obey its evil desires. Do not offer any part of yourself to sin as an instrument of wickedness, but rather offer yourselves to God as those who have been brought from death to life; and offer every part of yourself to him as an instrument of righteousness.**

Romans 6:11-13

When we consider ourselves dead to sin, we confess and walk in life by the Spirit. We say, "No, I cannot do this today. I have died to sin. It has no power over me."

One will ask, "But aren't we still living in the flesh?" Yes, that's what the Bible means when it says that the flesh wages war against the spirit (Galatians 5:17). But even though we live in the flesh we are to consider ourselves dead to it. We are to believe in the work of Christ which says, **"because anyone who has died has been set free from sin"** (Romans 6:7). This is how we **"walk by the Spirit"** so we don't gratify the desires of the flesh (Galatians 5:16). We declare freedom from sin, not captivity to it.

Don't let the devil tell you that you're still a sinner and have a propensity to sin. You don't. Consider yourself dead to sin. You are righteous. Jesus lives in you. Do you imagine Jesus sinning? Then don't imagine yourself sinning. Stand firm in who you are as a new creation and you will walk in victory!

You've got a victory life in you if you're a believer! Perceive it!

## KEEP ON THE NEW MAN

The Bible calls Satan a thief. So once we put on the new man in Christ, we can be sure that Satan will want to steal that revelation from us. The following are some practical, biblical steps we can take to keep on the new man in Christ:

## Focus on God's Goodness and Rewards

For years, the main approach ministers have taken with preaching against sin is to talk about how bad it is and tell the people not to do it. While sin is certainly bad and separates people from the Lord, telling people how bad it is and not to do it don't necessarily empower them to overcome it.

What people need to hear about in order to walk in victory over sin is the goodness of God—how God rewards those who serve Him. For ultimately, it is the goodness of God that draws men to repentance (Romans 2:4).

When Joseph was tempted to have sex by Potiphar's wife, the Bible records:

**"But he refused. 'With me in charge,' he told her, 'my master does not concern himself with anything in the house; everything he owns he has entrusted to my care. No one is greater in this house than I am. My master has withheld nothing from me except you, because you are his wife. How then could I do such a wicked thing and sin against God?'"**

Genesis 39:8-9

In the middle of being tempted, the goodness of God was the first thing on Joseph's mind. He thought of how God had abundantly blessed him, prospered him and gave him favor with man. It wasn't that Joseph didn't think she was attractive or that he wasn't interested in having sex with her. No, Joseph kept his eyes on the goodness of God and it became his empowerment to conquer temptation.

The reason why people have such a hard time overcoming sin is because they constantly place their focus on the wrong things: work, friends, politics, sports, celebrity life, etc. When the temptation comes, they've set themselves up to fail because they haven't taken the time to think about the goodness of God once.

The best way to focus on God's goodness and rewards ensuring we overcome temptation is to do it intentionally. Don't wait until the point of temptation to start trying to think of things. Make a list of the promises of God and confess them over your life every day. Here's an example:

1. God will withhold no good thing from me (Psalm 84:11).
2. God will take me to the top in every area of life (Deuteronomy 28:13).
3. God will use me as a special utensil in His end-time plan (2 Timothy 2:20-21).

**View Sin for What It Is**

Also by focusing on God's rewards, it forced Joseph view sin for what it really is: a destiny stealer. He understood that if he were to sin, he would lose God's and his master's favor, which would mean forfeiting the plan of God for his life.

We will never conquer what we don't hate. Joseph said, **"How then could I do such a wicked thing and sin against God?"** He hated the thought of it. What we don't hate we'll allow to remain.

And what we allow to remain will develop to be a stronghold in our life and destroy our destiny. As Proverbs 5:22 explains, a man's sins are like ropes that catch and hold him.

The more personal you can make this revelation the better:

You will not conquer pornography if you don't hate it.

You will not conqueror alcohol if it's "no big deal" to you.

You will not conqueror lying if they're just "white lies" to you.

Sin is serious business. Although all sins can be forgiven, not all can be recovered from. Some sins ruin marriages completely. Some land you in prison. Other sins flat out kill you. This is why Satan is called a thief who comes to steal, kill and destroy (John 10:10).

View every temptation through the lens of Satan. It's not just something pleasurable that is a "no-no." Behind the pleasure is a devil that wants to destroy the plan of God for your life, kill you before your time, ruin your relationships and steal your heart from the Lord.

**Fight with the Word**

The Word is the **"sword of the Spirit"** (Ephesians 6:17). It is a tool, a weapon, God has given us to overcome temptation and walk in victory over sin.

When Jesus was tempted by the devil, He fought and resisted every temptation with the Word. In every recorded response to the devil, Jesus said, **"It is written…"** (Luke 4:1-13). The Word was what He used to come out on top.

By "fighting with the Word" we use the power that is in the Word of God to **"demolish arguments and every pretension that sets itself up against the knowledge of God"** (2 Corinthians 10:5). The arguments and pretenses are attempts by the devil to get us to make compromises on holiness. He'll send people to tell us things like, "If you drank instead of being so uptight you could get more people saved" or "If you leave your boyfriend now that you're saved you won't have a place to live."

But when we have taken the time to know the Word, we won't be deceived into making compromises that lead to our death. We'll say, "No, wine is a mocker. People need help from alcohol, not influence to do it. And I'm going to be one of those people God uses to liberate them!" Or we'll say, "No, I'm leaving my boyfriend because God supplies all my needs. His favor is on my life as I obey and serve Him. I'll end up with a better house and an anointed husband."

What is happening when we fight with the Word like this, is that we take our thoughts captive. 2 Corinthians 10:5 continues, **"and we take every thought to make it obedient to Christ."** We don't have to "allow" the temptation to rest in our minds. We can take it captive, not be its captive, by the Word. Instead of pondering about it, we can speak out the Word: "I will not do that for I am a child of God. I am destined for greatness. Christ is alive in me. I have died to sin, so it cannot be my master."

I believe it was Kenneth Hagin who once said, "You can't prevent a bird from flying over your head, but you can prevent it from making a nest in your hair." We might not be able to control what comes into our minds, but we can certainly take those thoughts captive when they do come by fighting with the Word. We don't have to let them make nests in our minds.

**Prayer**

Praying, especially in the Holy Spirit, builds us up (Jude 1:20). It increases our strength and faith to live how God desires we live.

On one occasion when Jesus was with the disciples, He rebuked them for their lack of prayer, saying, **"Watch and pray so that you will not fall into temptation. The spirit is willing, but the flesh is weak"** (Matthew 26:41). Jesus warned that prayerlessness would be there downfall.

Prayerlessness produces powerlessness. Even when we know what we ought to do, a lack of prayer on our part will result in a lack of power on our part to walk righteously.

On the opposite end of the spectrum, prayer-*fullness* produces power-*fullness*. Jesus was *always* praying and He never lacked power. He did not sin—ever. And so if we are careful to be prayer-*full*, we will remain power-*full*. Like Jesus, we will not sin, for **"Christ lives in you"** (Colossians 1:27 NLT). If we pray like He prayed, we will receive the power that He received.

How often should we be praying? In the passage above, Jesus rebuked them for not being able to pray for even an hour (Matthew 26:40). So it would certainly be appropriate to set a standard at praying no less than one hour each day.

Make a commitment to praying every day and you can be sure to walk in power every day to live righteously.

**Be Consumed with Your Purpose**

Perhaps the main reason that David committed adultery with Bathsheba was that he had stopped pressing forward in his purpose. The Bible records:

**In the spring, at the time when kings go off to war, David sent Joab out with the king's men and the whole Israelite army. They destroyed the Ammonites and besieged Rabbah. But David remained in Jerusalem.**

2 Samuel 11:1

He was at home when he should've been at war. If he would've been at war, consumed with his purpose, he would have never even seen Bathsheba on the rooftop.

Idleness opens the door for sin. If we are consumed with the purpose God has given us, we won't have time or energy to get involved in the sins of the world. We'll be so busy and happy doing the work of God, we won't even have the chance to see a "Bathsheba."

Yet more than merely being distracted so we don't sin, we tap into supernatural power when we consume ourselves with our purpose.

In John 4, Jesus' disciples urged Him to eat, but He responded by saying, **"I have food to eat that you know nothing about"** (John 4:32). At this, the disciples were utterly confused because they hadn't seen Him eat anything. So Jesus explained, **"My food is to do the will of him who sent me..."** (John 4:34). In other words, His strength and energy came from fulfilling His purpose!

As we consume ourselves with God's plan for our lives, we'll realize that instead of getting tired, we get more energized—energized for the things of God and to live righteously. Instead of sin's pleasures fueling us, God's pleasures fuel us. We rid ourselves of the desire for sin because we're not reinforcing and empowering it. We are draining the strength of its pull as God's purpose for our lives pushes onward.

*CHAPTER 5*

# LIVING WITH HEALING POWER

Jesus was never sick. He healed the sick. Since we are called to be like Jesus in every way, healing is God's will for every believer.

Believing that God *can* heal is rarely the issue. Many believers know that God is able. If God *will* heal is the question that needs answered for us to walk in healing.

As we discussed in the chapter Faith to Be and Do, believing that God is able is not sufficient for healing. It will leave the believer wondering about his specific situation. And if there is question in his mind about what God will do, there is doubt, and where there is doubt, there is not faith. So, we must be thoroughly convinced that it is God's will to heal each person.

## SICKNESS IS SATAN'S WILL

Healing and prosperity (which we will deal with in the next chapter) seem to be the only aspects of God's will where people stumble. Few question if God will forgive them. Few question if God loves them. Few question if God will guide them. Yet in the Bible, God's will to heal is demonstrated just as clearly as His will to forgive and love and guide. This mixed-up mindset is not mere coincidence. For in the scriptures, it is abundantly clear that Satan is the author of sickness. Sickness is Satan's will.

Satan wants people to believe that sickness is God's will or that it is "allowed" by God because he knows it causes confusion about the Lord's goodness. People who have lost a loved one to sickness often ask, "If God is so good, why didn't God heal my son?" Since many churches do not believe in healing, the only response they get is, "Well, sometimes we don't know why God does what He does, we just have to trust Him."

Of course, these people develop a bitterness toward God and do not serve Him. And I don't blame them. That kind of god is not good. I like how T.L Osborn once put it: "If God can't do miracles, why call him God? If God can do miracles but won't, he's not as good as I am because I would if I could. But thank God, he's better than me. He can and he will.[4]"

Moreover, if the devil can stop us from walking in victory, he can stop us from living as liberators so others can see victory in their lives. We won't believe God wills to heal us, so how could we ever believe for God to heal someone else? We won't.

The following sections explain how sickness is Satan's will:

**Sin and Sickness Have the Same Origin**

When God made mankind in the Garden of Eden, He made them as healthy beings. He did not make them with sickness. Adam and Eve did not have cancer or poor eyesight.

Sickness and death came as a result of the Fall of Man. And Satan was the author of the Fall (Genesis 3:1-7). He was the Deceiver (2 Corinthians 11:3-14). It was his will to get Adam and Eve to sin, for he knew full well the destruction it would bring to their lives. When sin entered, death, sickness, pain and suffering entered. So because sickness entered in with sin, they have the same origin: they are both from the devil.

We also find the following dynamic all through the scriptures: sin and sickness are often linked, whereas forgiveness and healing are often linked. That link is never reversed. Healing is always considered a blessing of righteousness, while sickness is always considered a curse of sin—a work of Satan:

- See the following scriptures for reference of the link between forgiveness and healing: Numbers 21:4-9, Deuteronomy 28:1-14, 2 Chronicles 7:14, Psalm 103:1-5, Proverbs 3:7-8, Isaiah 1:4-6, Isaiah 33:24, Matthew 9:5-7, James 5:14-15, 3 John 1:2.
- See the following scriptures for reference of the link between sin and sickness: Leviticus 26:16, Numbers 21:4-9, Deuteronomy 28:15-68, Lamentations 3:33-42, Job 33:19-27, Psalm 119:67-71, John 5:14, Acts 5:1-11, Acts 13:8-11, 1 Corinthians 11:27-34.

Of course, sickness is not always linked to sin as Jesus explained in John 9 to the crowd about a man born blind: **"'Neither this man nor his parents sinned,' said Jesus, 'but this happened so that the works of God might be displayed in him'"** (John 9:3).

We must be careful in our interpretation here. God did not make him blind. Acts 10:38 tells us that Jesus **"went around doing good and healing all who were under the power of the devil, because God was with him"** (Acts 10:38). The man was under the power of the devil. The devil made him blind. What Jesus meant by **"but this happened"** was that it was God's will, His purpose, in the sickness to bring healing. For if sickness was God's will, this man would not have been healed. He would've stayed blind. Nor did Jesus said he was blind because he had to learn something. No. The only thing that mattered was that God desired healing for this man.

God's purpose in any attack of the devil is always victory or healing. If the bad in people's lives remains bad, God obtains no glory. God hadn't received an ounce of glory through the man in John 9 being blind. In fact, the only thing glorified all those years was Satan because everyone had attributed his blindness to sin, which is a work of Satan. Rather, God only received glory once the man was healed. The same is true for us. If we stay sick, God obtains no glory. Healing brings Him glory.

**Jesus' Attitude Toward Sickness**

In every case of sickness that Jesus encountered, He treated the sickness the same way He treated demons: He cast them out. Luke

4:39 says, **"So he bent over her and rebuked the fever, and it left her. She got up at once and began to wait on them."**

Not once did Jesus tell people to tolerate their sickness. He did not tell people that their sickness was God's will or that God was trying to teach them something. He always attacked the sickness head on and commanded it to leave people's bodies.

If sickness is the will of God or a result of the hand of God, Jesus would have been casting Himself out of people, for He was anointed *by* God (Acts 10:38, Luke 4:18-19). And if God drives out God, He is divided against Himself. He is working against Himself. As Jesus taught, how could such a kingdom stand (Matthew 12:22-28)? On the contrary, Jesus received an anointing to heal:

**"The Spirit of the Lord is on me, because he has anointed me to proclaim good news to the poor. He has sent me to proclaim freedom for the prisoners and recovery of sight for the blind, to set the oppressed free…"**

Luke 4:18

Jesus also attacked sickness when he commissioned his disciples. When he sent them out to preach, He also sent them out to heal the sick:

**As you go, proclaim this message: 'The kingdom of heaven has come near.' Heal the sick, raise the dead, cleanse those who have leprosy, drive out demons. Freely you have received; freely give.**

Matthew 10:7-8

Preaching is for all, it is not conditional. Jesus never said, "Go preach to some so some can be saved." No, Jesus said, "Go preach to all so all can be saved." And if preaching is for all, but healing is not for all, it makes no sense why would Jesus lump preaching and healing together. Yet the disciples were to heal when and where they preached.

**Our Calling to Heal the Sick**

Healing was not only linked with preaching for the disciples, but it is also linked with preaching for us today. In Mark 16, Jesus commissioned *every* believer to preach the Gospel, heal the sick and perform signs and wonders. All authority over sickness and disease has been given to us (Luke 10:19).

God pit us against sickness just as He did Jesus and the early church. It is our enemy, for it is of the devil. If sickness were God's will for us and God made people sick, sickness would be our friend, not enemy. And if we tried to heal people, we would be healing them from *God*. Even as Jesus said in Mark 12:22-28, a house that is divided against itself cannot stand, for it destroys itself. If we cast out God by the power of God, God's kingdom is divided against itself. Sickness, then, is not of God but of Satan.

Since it is of Satan, sickness is not something we must cope with or something we must comfort others through. Just like sin, it is something we are called to destroy in other's lives. We must view it with the same hatred as we do Satan himself.

Like the devil, sickness is a thief and murderer (John 10:10). It takes the life, energy and resources from people. It separates families by killing young children, fathers, mothers and siblings. In cases even when the afflicted people do not die, it prevents them from living out God's purpose for their lives by making them bed-ridden and too weak. Or, it plunges people into financial ruin because of the expense of doctors and treatments. Sickness is in no way, shape or form good. Visit your local cancer ward. It is utterly evil and should be treated as such.

## HEALING IS GOD'S WILL

In direct opposition of the will of Satan to make sick is God's will to heal. Let us discuss those truths:

**God's Eternal Character**

In Exodus 15:26, after the Israelites were rescued out of Egypt, God told them that He would not bring on them the diseases He inflicted on their oppressors, but that He would heal them. He said, **"For I am the Lord, who heals you."**

This is one of God's "I am" declarations existent in the Bible. The original language essentially reads, "I am Yahweh Rapha," which means "the Lord who heals." In other words, this wasn't God saying that He would heal on this occasion, this was God giving insight into His character. He was saying that healing is who He *is*.

He *is* a healer.

In Malachi 3:6, God tells us that He never changes. If we say that healing is no longer God's will, we are saying that God has changed. That cannot be. There was not a "day of miracles." There is only a God of miracles. The only option is to conclude that healing is still very much His will for today.

**The Life of Jesus**

Jesus was sent to do and be the express will of the Father. He said in John 5:19, **"Very truly I tell you, the Son can do nothing by himself; he can do only what he sees his Father doing, because whatever the Father does the Son also does."** Therefore, everything Jesus did was because God Himself does it, and everything He didn't do was because God didn't do it.

What did Jesus do? He healed. Acts 10:38 says, **"how God anointed Jesus of Nazareth with the Holy Spirit and power, and how he went around doing good and healing all who were under the power of the devil, because God was with him."** Jesus healed because it is God's will to heal.

What did Jesus never do? He never put sickness on people. He never turned people away from healing. He didn't give the crippled canes. He didn't recommend the sick to doctors.

No, Jesus healed. In fact, healing power *flowed* from Him and healed everyone coming to Him: **"and the people all tried to touch him, because power was coming from him and healing them all"** (Luke 6:19). It was available to all and healing them all just as anyone can jump in a river.

One may say that Jesus' healings were only to prove that He was the Messiah and that nowadays we have the scriptures to believe in and don't need miracles. But that's only half true.

First, the Bible also tells us that Jesus healed because of His compassion for the sick (Matthew 9:36). So I ask, does Jesus have less compassion for the sick today? By no means! **"Jesus Christ the same yesterday, and to day, and forever"** (Hebrews 13:8 KJV). For **"the Lord is good to all; he has compassion on all he has made"** (Psalm 145:9). Jesus looks on the sick today from His seat in heaven with the same level of compassion and readiness to heal as He did on earth.

Second, the Bible also tells us that Jesus healed because it was the right of God's children—the children of Abraham. On one occasion after Jesus healed a woman's back, He said, **"Then should not this woman, a daughter of Abraham, whom Satan has kept bound for eighteen long years, be set free on the Sabbath day from what bound her?"** (Luke 13:16). It was her status as a child of Abraham that warranted her healing.

On another occasion, speaking to a Canaanite woman about healing for her daughter, Jesus said, **"It is not right to take the children's bread and toss it to the dogs"** (Matthew 15:26). He referred to healing as the children's bread. Which children? Those of Abraham's seed. It was their bread, their rightful, daily nourishment. Jesus considered it awful to not give it to them.

Are not we who believe in Christ also called sons of Abraham? Should not healing belong to us as it did to them? Absolutely!

Galatians 3:9 says, **"So those who rely on faith are blessed along with Abraham, the man of faith."** Galatians 3:13 and Galatians 3:19 draw the same conclusion as well.

Let us also remember that the life of Jesus has been imparted to us. Christ lives in us. We are called to be Jesus to this world—liberators of the sinful, sick, broken and needy. We are not called to be strugglers. Healing *must* be God's will for us for this reason alone. If healing was not for us, we would end up being too sick to heal the sick. Thank God healing is for us, not only for our sakes, but so everyone else can be healed as well!

**Healing through the Atonement**

Isaiah 53:4-5, a prophecy of Jesus' redemptive work, tells us:

**Surely he took up our pain and bore our suffering, yet we considered him punished by God, stricken by him, and afflicted. But he was pierced for our transgressions, he was crushed for our iniquities; the punishment that brought us peace was on him, and by his wounds we are healed.**

Jesus bore our sufferings, pains and sicknesses in the same sacrifice when He bore our sins. It was on the cross that He bore our sins, but it was by the stripes He took that He bore our sicknesses. Sin was dealt with by the cross; sickness was dealt with by the stripes.

That is why under the Old Covenant the sacrificial lambs were not beaten. They were killed, but not whipped. Our sacrificial lamb called Jesus, however, *was* beaten. For it is God's will that we be made whole both in spirit and body.

Some argue that Isaiah 53 talks about spiritual healing rather than physical. However, in the Gospel of Matthew this scripture is referenced by its writer within the context of physical healing. Matthew 8:16-17:

**"When evening came, many who were demon-possessed were brought to him, and he drove out the spirits with a word and healed all the sick. This was to fulfill what was spoken through the prophet Isaiah: 'He took up our infirmities and bore our diseases.'"**

If spiritual healing was what God meant in Isaiah, then a *physical* healing would not have fulfilled the prophecy. Matthew would have needed to reference Isaiah 53 for Jesus forgiving someone, not after healing someone. "By his wounds we are healed" must mean physical healing.

And since physical healing is a part of redemption which is for all people (Titus 2:11), healing is for all people. We do not ever have to be sick. Just as Jesus bearing our sins means that we need not bear them, Jesus bearing our sicknesses means that we need not bear them.

Additionally, some claim that we might not be healed because "we live in a fallen world." But the promise of healing was given *to* the fallen world, not some imaginary world that never existed without the presence of sin and sickness. The entire purpose of redemption was to *redeem* the fallen world. Galatians 3:13, **"Christ redeemed us from the curse of the law by becoming a curse for us, for it is written: 'Cursed is everyone who is hung on a pole.'"**

The curse of the Law, as defined in Deuteronomy 27:26, included the curses that followed in Deuteronomy 28. Among them is every sickness on the face of the earth (Deuteronomy 28:61). Through Christ, we are redeemed from these curses! Healing is ours! We don't ever "have" to be sick.

"But there is a devil" doesn't negate the Word of God, either. Is it true that the devil may try to make us sick? Yes, but it doesn't suddenly make sickness God's will. It doesn't undo what Jesus did on the cross.

The Bible calls Satan a thief (John 10:10). By nature, thieves try to take what they are not supposed to take. If a thief comes to our home to steal our TV, for instance, we don't let it happen and say, "Well, maybe that TV isn't for me." No! It still belongs to us. We go after it and get it.

The same is true with respect to healing. We don't say, "I guess I have to be sick" or "I guess healing isn't for me" if Satan tries to steal our healing or attack our bodies with sickness. No! We say, "This sickness is not mine. Jesus bore it! Sickness be gone in the name of Jesus!" We don't stop confessing the Word just because the devil attacked us. Quite the contrary! We confess it all the more! We believe it all the more! When we stand on the Word in faith like that, healing in inevitable.

## HEALING BY FAITH

Looking back to the scripture in Matthew 6:19, it was not merely the people's "going" to Jesus that accessed His healing power. It was their going to Him in faith. For Jesus could and can only heal in response to faith.

In Mark 6:5 and Matthew 13:58 we find where Jesus could not perform any miracles in his hometown except heal just a few people because of the town's unbelief. Unbelief hindered *Jesus* from healing the sick. If divine healing has nothing to do with faith and solely relies on God's random sovereignty, as is largely taught today, why didn't Jesus just heal all of them in the scriptures above? If healing is through God's will irrespective of faith, *all* of the people would have been healed because Christ was clearly willing. He was explicitly *trying* to heal the sick. But He was unable because of *their* unbelief.

Jesus is just as willing to heal us today as He was on earth. The reason why people fail to receive healing today is much the same as it was with Jesus' hometown of Nazareth: they rejected Him—the Word. People have come to believe their own ideas about healing instead of what God's Word plainly says. As a result, they don't have faith because they're believing something not in the Word.

Teaching people the Word is precisely what Jesus did in response to Nazareth's unbelief: **"He was amazed at their lack of faith. Then Jesus went around teaching from village to village"** (Mark 6:6). He didn't say, "Oh well, sometimes people don't get healed and that's how it is." No, He was stirred to teach them the Word so they could receive faith and be healed.

In fact, this run-in with an entire town's lack of faith was why Jesus commissioned His disciples. He realized that there needed to be more people teaching and preaching the Word—specifically in the matter of healing! The very next verses read: **"Calling the Twelve to him, he began to send them out two by two and gave them authority over impure spirits...They drove out many demons and anointed many sick people with oil and healed them"** (Mark 6:7-13).

Today, people have "gone to God" for healing knowing full well what He is able to do but have been taught that sometimes God is not willing to. This is the ultimate faith destroyer that must be corrected with the truth of the Word. God is willing! Let us refuse to believe otherwise.

## BAD TEACHINGS & ANSWERS TO QUESTIONS

For someone who has sat under a lot of unscriptural teachings, God's will to heal *everyone* can be hard to grasp. Since I haven't always believed this way but now do—in fact, I used to argue until blue in the face against the idea—I have already had the chance to work through the questions and supposedly contradictory theology. So in the following sections, it is my goal to provide scriptural clarity in those question areas:

**God's Will to Heal is Not Based on Experience**

Perhaps the most common argument people make against God's

will to heal all people is with experience. For example, someone will have had an aunt who loved God very much yet died of cancer, which is their reason for not believing God heals everyone. They will say, "Are you saying my aunt, who loved God sincerely, did not have faith?" In essence, they are using experience to dictate truth instead of the Word.

When Tabitha who was **"always doing good and helping the poor"** (Acts 9:36) died from sickness, the Apostle Peter didn't say, "Well, I guess we had this whole thing wrong. She was a genuine believer. Everyone could see it. It must've been God's will that she remain sick and die." No! Not even sickness to the point of death was a good enough experience to invalidate God's Word. Peter sent everyone who was crying out of the room, prayed, and said, **"Tabitha, get up"** (Acts 9:40). And she sat up, alive, back from the dead!

The moment we start allowing our experiences to dictate what the Word of God means is the moment we step into trouble. This is why Peter was able to perform a miracle. He refused to let someone's experience dictate what he believed, what Jesus had told him.

So if when explaining what we believe, we start with, "Well, I believe…" instead of "The Bible says…" that is an indication we're believing based on our experiences instead of the Word. We must then realign our thinking and believing to be Word-based. That takes swallowing pride and admitting we have been wrong, possibly for decades. But we ought to do so in joy because we're receiving clarity on the Word of God! That's a wonderful thing because it enables us to walk in God's wonderful promises!

Imagine if we used experience to determine if salvation is real as so many have done with healing. Countless people have heard the Gospel and did not believe. I have even had people say to me, "I've tried Jesus and it just doesn't work for me." Yet we don't discount salvation just because of the experience of some. We don't say that the new creation isn't real just because some believers fell back into sin. No! We believe the Word anyways! So should our understanding be when it comes to divine healing.

### God's Will to Heal is not Based on People's Ability to Walk in the Authority to Heal

I know of some people who are convinced that healing is not God's will for everyone because their family member was "even prayed for by T.L. Osborn, the great healing evangelist" and did not recover from the illness.

We must be careful to understand that God's will to heal is not based on people's ability to walk in the authority Christians received from Jesus to heal the sick. Our faith must rest in God's will, not in people's ability to carry it out.

The Bible records that not even the *disciples* were able to heal a young boy on one instance. This event is found in Matthew 17. The boy's father said to Jesus, **"I brought him to your disciples, but they could not heal him"** (Matthew 17:16). Of course, Jesus—because it is God's will—went on to heal the boy. Jesus did not say, "Since they couldn't do it, that means it isn't God's will."

If not even the disciples were able to walk flawlessly in the authority to heal, we today must refuse to base God's will to heal upon people's ability to carry it out. We are all aiming to be like Christ in every way. If we fall short, God's will to heal remains the same nonetheless.

**Reliance on "Wisdom"**

Let us look back to Jesus' life to see *how* He healed. He healed people by God's power. He did not recommend people to doctors. He did not give the crippled wheelchairs. It was by the anointing power of God that they were healed.

Most churches today have relegated divine healing to nothing more than, "We believe God uses doctors." Now, they will self-proclaim that they believe in divine healing, too (the church I grew up in did, at least), but when hard pressed about actual miracles, they likely can't furnish even one. So basically, they just believe in doctors as God's method of healing.

God using doctors to heal people is an idea found nowhere in the Bible. One may ask, "But wasn't Luke a physician?" Yes, and there isn't a single instance in scripture where Jesus or Paul had to use him. That's because God's will to heal is independent of doctors and medicine. He is the healer.

It is a mistake when people zero-in on Paul telling Timothy to drink a little wine for the sake of Timothy's frequent stomach ailments (1 Timothy 5:23) as an example of God using doctors. Paul's instruction to Timothy was over bad drinking water—that is how it must be contextually understood. So arguing that this scripture has any say in determining the clear doctrine of divine healing Paul demonstrated through the rest of his life and ministry is intellectual dishonesty. One involves hygienic, the other involves making crippled people walk. Paul never said to the crippled, "Here's a wheelchair from God for your healing," or "Be sure to take your seizure medication."

To such, people will retort, "That's ridiculous. We have to use wisdom." So I ask, "Is your human wisdom is higher than God's? Is God, who says, **"And the prayer offered in faith will make the sick person well"** (James 5:15) passing out unwise advice, then? Quite the contrary! There isn't "faith" and then "wisdom." They are not mutually exclusive. Faith is the *highest* form of wisdom because it rests not in the wisdom of men but of God. This is what the Word of God means when it says, **"Trust in the Lord with all your heart and lean not on your own understanding"** (Proverbs 3:5). God has said He would heal us by His power, so believing Him is the wisest thing a person could ever do.

It's not that doctors and man's wisdom are wrong or sinful. Remember, if it was *not* God's will to heal people, going to a doctor *would* be sinful because we would be working against His will. The problem is with faith.

First, adding doctors to God's will to heal raises the question, who *really* are people putting their faith and trust in? When a believer who doesn't understand divine healing gets sick, he will inevitably go to a doctor to seek healing. If the doctor can help them, they raise their hands and thank God for His healing. But if the doctor can't heal them, they decide that it must not be God's will to heal them.

Notice that the person didn't discover God's will for them through the Word. No, they discovered it through the doctor, through man's wisdom. So the believer isn't placing faith in God—they're literally not looking to God (His Word) at all! They think they are trusting in God, but the entire grounds for what they'll decide to believe is based on what a *man* can or cannot do.

Matthew 19:26 declares, **"With man this is impossible, but with God all things are possible."** There are limits to man but there are no limits to God! We serve an unlimited God! So we don't want to limit God by limiting Him to what mankind can achieve. Jesus tells us, **"If thou canst believe, all things are possible to him that believeth"** (Mark 9:23 KJV). If *you* can believe it, God can do it!

Second, adding doctors to God's will to heal doesn't facilitate an exercise or growth of faith. At the first sign of a cold, believers run to a doctor and get medicine instead of exercising faith and taking authority over the sickness. But then if later in life they get diagnosed with cancer, they suddenly want to believe God for supernatural healing. That's like trying to bench press 400 pounds when you've never even been to the gym before.

What we should be doing is going to God first, exercising faith in James 5:14-15, Acts 10:38 and the other healing scriptures, and starting with small things. You don't have to immediately go out and raise the dead—unless that's where your faith is, of course. Then, as we start exercising faith in small things, we will grow our faith to believe for even great things! And I don't speak of *us* getting healed, I speak of God using us to heal *others*!

Bishop David Oyedepo, in his book Exploits in Ministry, calls this adhering to the law of absolute dependency on God[5]. We should cultivate in ourselves the understanding that if God can't do it, give it to us or take us there, we should let it remain undone. This means refusing to create a backup plan in our hearts while "trying" to believe God.

Decide today that you are going to believe God! You are going to be a person of faith!

**God Teaches by Instruction not Destruction**

Some people teach that sickness and misfortune in general are God's will in that sometimes He teaches through them. They explain that they prayed for healing but nothing happened, so they suppose that God wants to teach them a lesson or refine them spiritually through the sickness.

However, God has expressed that it is His will to teach through His Word, not through sickness and suffering. Psalm 94:12 says, **"Blessed is the one you discipline, Lord, the one you teach from your law; you grant them relief from days of trouble…"** God's discipline means being taught from His word. Like a teacher, He has an instruction manual which is His Word. As 2 Timothy 3:16-17 explains, **"All Scripture is God-breathed and is useful for teaching, rebuking, correcting and training in righteousness, so that the servant of God may be thoroughly equipped for every good work."**

The reason why such person is called "blessed" in Psalm 94 is because it results in relief from trouble, not causes trouble. The scripture implies that the whole reason why God wants to give us instruction is to prevent suffering.

Proverbs 4:20-22 tells us: **"My son, pay attention to what I say; turn your ear to my words. Do not let them out of your sight, keep them within your heart; for they are life to those who find them and health to one's whole body."** By listening to God's instructions, we encounter life and health—blessings. Yet those who claim that God teaches with sickness or suffering *never* call themselves blessed. They say, "I am suffering" not "I am blessed." And rightly so—sickness and suffering are not blessings.

Ignoring God's instructions or ignorance of them is what causes people to experience trouble in their lives. As Isaiah 48:17-18 says:

**"…I am the Lord your God, who teaches you what is best for you, who directs you in the way you should go. If only you had paid attention to my commands, your peace would have been like a river, your well-being like the waves of the sea."**

God's best way meant peace and a good well-being, but because the Israelites ignored what God had told them to do they suffered.

The scripture for the confusion about how God teaches is generally Hebrews 12:7 which says, **"Endure hardship as discipline; God is treating you as his children. For what children are not disciplined by their father?"**

In response, first, there is a difference between hardship and sickness. We will teach on this in a later chapter. However, we will suffice to say that hardship always calls for perseverance, while sickness always calls for healing (James 1:2-4, James 5:13-16). We are not ever in scripture called to endure sickness.

Second, the context of Hebrews 12 is about sin, and specifically against enduring against sinning (Hebrews 12:4). The NASB interprets verse 7 more correctly in accordance with the context, saying, **"It is for discipline that you endure..."** meaning, again, enduring against sin. God is saying, "As you struggle against sin, get convicted and have to repent, consider it discipline for the sake of righteousness. The idea of "hardship" is not associated with any of the words in the original language in this verse.

In its interpretation, the KJV orders the syntax of the original language slightly different, producing, **"If ye endure chastening..."** Chasten means discipline for wrongdoing. So in this interpretation, the scripture discusses the Lord disciplining people for sinning—just as a father chastens his children for doing something *wrong*. Thus, this interpretation is very close to that of the NASB and involves no idea of hardship, either.

Also, the first time the thought and point of Hebrews 12:7 was ever expressed was to the Israelites in Deuteronomy 8:2-5 and it involved the matter of sin:

**Remember how the Lord your God led you all the way in the wilderness these forty years, to humble and test you in order to know what was in your heart, whether or not you would keep his commands. He humbled you, causing you to hunger and then feeding you with manna, which neither you nor your**

**ancestors had known, to teach you that man does not live on bread alone but on every word that comes from the mouth of the Lord. Your clothes did not wear out and your feet did not swell during these forty years. Know then in your heart that as a man disciplines his son, so the Lord your God disciplines you.**

God had to discipline and test the Israelites because of sin and unbelief (Numbers 14:20-35). If they had believed they could conquer the land of Canaan, they would have possessed it and would not have spent a single day in the wilderness. So discipline **"as a man disciplines his son"** doesn't merely mean because the father so feels like giving his son some hardship, it directly implies the need for discipline because of actions his son had taken.

While sickness may certainly be a consequence of sin (John 5:14), to say that God "uses" it is scripturally wrong. The Bible teaches that we reap what we sow: **"Do not be deceived: God cannot be mocked. A man reaps what he sows. Whoever sows to please their flesh, from the flesh will reap destruction…"** (Galatians 6:7-8). It is not God using sickness to teach us a lesson; rather, it is the consequence of our mistake causing us to rethink our actions. Such is the case when a parent tells a child not to touch a hot stove. If the child doesn't listen and touches it anyways, we do not say that it was the parent's need or will for the child to do so in order to learn to not do it. No, the child simply learned from his actions. In the same way, God uses His Word and Holy Spirit to teach us things and grow us spiritually, not sickness.

**What About Death?**

"If healing is God's will, how are we supposed to die?"

Every human being must die. Hebrews 9:27 (KJV) tells us that **"it is appointed unto men once to die, but after this the judgement."**

However, it is God's will that we live a long, satisfying life. The Bible says, **"With long life I will satisfy him and show him my salvation"** (Psalm 91:16). Notice how God links salvation with a long life. Living a long life is necessary in order for us to experience salvation to its fullest!

It's not God's will when a child dies of leukemia. Children are to grow old and be mighty warriors for God (Psalm 112:2). It's not His will when a middle-aged parent dies of a heart attack. Each parent is to become old and gray, declaring God's power to the next generation (Psalm 71:18).

When it is our time to die, it does not have to be a mystery. Jesus knew when it was His time to go (Matthew 16:21, Matthew 26:45). He freely laid down His life (John 10:18), it was not taken from Him by disaster or disease. He walked right through crowds as if invisible when they tried to kill Him (Luke 4:29-30).

Another example is found in Paul. Paul knew when it was his time to die (2 Timothy 4:6-8). He also knew when it *wasn't* his time to die (Philippians 1:20-25). Just as with Jesus, he was not taken out by disease or disaster. Even when he encountered the storm on the ocean in Acts 27, an angel confirmed that he was not to die because he had to go to Rome, just as God had previously revealed to him

(Acts 23:11). In the end, Paul laid down his life to persecution like Jesus (Acts 21:13).

There is a plan for our lives, which runs into old age, that must be completed before we can go on to heaven. Paul said, **"I have finished the race"** (2 Timothy 4:7). No sickness, storm or persecution can take us out until that time. It's not until we finish the race that we'll reach our end.

## EVANGELISM VS. EMPATHY

We are called to be liberators, which includes healing the sick—placing our hands on them for healing or rebuking the sickness. By doing so we evangelize the world, making known the love and power of Jesus.

We are not called to empathize. That is, God does not use *our* sicknesses so other people can come to Christ. We are called to heal the sick. And empathy does not get people healed. No amount of empathy stirs up God's healing anointing. Rather, it takes someone who understands they have been given all authority over sickness and disease to be anointed to command healing into the bodies of the sick (Ephesians 1:18-20).

Being able to empathize with people's feelings and situations is certainly helpful, but empathy is not evangelism; nor is empathy necessary. For saying that God has us sick so we can relate to sick people and win them to Christ is like saying God has us addicted to heroin so we can win drug addicts to Christ.

An empathy approach to evangelism is why AA meetings are

unsuccessful: people who have had drinking problems for years giving "advice" to people who also have drinking problems. It is also why the "dirty Christian" mentality taught in churches is unsuccessful and blatantly unscriptural. They'll say, "We're just sinners helping sinners." Helping them do what, exactly? You can't "help" sin, you get free. And if neither of you are free, you are simply comforting each other on the road to destruction! As the Bible says, **"If the blind lead the blind, both will fall into a pit"** (Matthew 15:14). You can't help people if you yourself need help.

Of course, a previous addict can lead someone to Christ. And one who was an addict can certainly better relate to that person's pains. But it's not our current struggles that lead people to Christ—it is our victory over the struggle because of the truth from God's Word we received and applied to our lives. That's called a testimony. For the gospel is the power of God unto salvation, not our ability to empathize.

God does not need us to be sick any more than He needs us to be sinful to see the lost saved. He does not give us sickness or "use" our sicknesses—it's His will we be healed! More than that, it's our calling to be like Jesus and heal the sick! If the Lord needs one of His children to be sick, He breaks His promise of healing to them and prevents them from fulfilling His command to them to be liberators for others.

What God needs are people who believe what His Word says in that that they are called to be liberators and who go out and preach the Gospel with signs following.

I see you being one of those people in Jesus name!

*CHAPTER 6*

# LIVING OUT FINANCIAL PROSPERITY

Perhaps the most success the devil has had in deceiving believers has been in the realm of money. He has convinced countless people, churches and denominations that prosperity is heresy. The very mention of the word "prosperity" for many believers is like fingernails on a chalk board.

It is certainly true that the prosperity message has been abused. However, the existence of an abuse in one case—or even many—in itself does not invalidate truthfulness. Truth is truth regardless of how people act according to it.

What we must be aware of is that the devil works through offense to get us to miss out on revelation from the Word. The Bible tells us that the entrance of God's Word brings light (Psalm 119:130). Light means understanding about the will of God. If the devil can get us to be offended at the preaching of the Word because it's not how we were raised to believe or because the minister turned out to be a fraud, we'll turn away from the Word. We'll take our focus off the

Word and onto the offense. As a result, we will not see what God wants us to see—for His Word brings light. It lights up what He wants us to see, know and understand.

This is why many God-loving, God-fearing people have missed out on what God has to say about prosperity. They've dug their heels in and don't even care to hear scripture on the subject because of past offenses and refuse to listen to scripture on the matter. And since our ability to stand firm in life comes from hearing and doing the Word (Luke 6:46-49), such people will suffer defeat in their finances. They won't know what the Word says about prosperity, so they will not see victory in that area of their lives.

As we look to the Word who is Jesus with an open heart free from the corruption of religion, we discover that it is God's will for us to walk victory in every area of our lives, including finances.

## GOD'S VIEW OF POVERTY

Galatians 3:13 tells us, **"Christ redeemed us from the curse of the law by becoming a curse for us, for it is written: 'Cursed is everyone who is hung on a pole.'"** What is the curse of the Law? This is where the Old Testament comes in to play. From the end of Deuteronomy 27 and into Deuteronomy 28, scripture tells us that Curse of the Law are curses because of disobedience to God's commands. Essentially, they are curses because of sin.

A large majority of the curses listed involve poverty and lack. For instance, verse 38 says, **"You will sow much seed in the field but you will harvest little."** That means working hard at our careers but never bringing home enough, always being in a state of need.

Since poverty is listed in the "curses" half of the chapter, God deems poverty as a curse—a self-evident truth. He does not call it good. That is why He sent His son Jesus Christ to *redeem* us from it as Galatians 3:13 stated. Redeemed means rescued.

Anyone who has ever been poor or suffered a financial setback understands that poverty is a curse. It's horrible not having enough to feed our children. It's horrible having our home taken away because we lost our job and couldn't afford the payments. It's horrible losing everything we own in a fire. It's horrible not being able to afford college or to pursue the dream God has given us.

Yet all too often, religion twists scriptures to make money out to be the curse and poverty the blessing from God. Religious people will say, "It was because I lost everything that I found Jesus." No, it was because someone preached you the Gospel that you found Jesus. For the *Gospel* is the power of God unto salvation (Romans 1:16), *not* complete destruction and loss.

Since God deems poverty and lack a curse, we ought to recognize them as curses. We have to lose any religious mentality which makes prosperity out to be the curse instead of poverty.

If prosperity was the curse (the result of disobedience), the patriarchs would all be in hell because they were all very wealthy:

Abraham was **"very wealthy in livestock and in silver and gold"** (Genesis 13:2). Isaac was very wealthy: **"The man became rich, and his wealth continued to grow until he became very wealthy"** (Genesis 26:13). Jacob was exceedingly prosperous (Genesis 30:43).

Again, since they were very wealthy, if prosperity were the curse it would mean that they would have been very sinful. This is not the case.

Jesus did not redeem us from prosperity. We do not see anywhere in the Bible where God blessed people by giving them poverty or by destroying everything they own. No, the blessing of God is always linked to prosperity, and poverty is always linked to being a curse. Proverbs 10:22 (NLT) says, **"The blessing of the Lord brings wealth, without painful toil for it."**

## GOD'S REMEDY IS PROSPERITY

God's remedy for poverty is prosperity through Jesus Christ. The Bible tells us in 2 Corinthians 8:9: **"For you know the grace of our Lord Jesus Christ, that though he was rich, yet for your sake he became poor, so that you through his poverty might become rich."** This does not mean spiritual "richness" but financial overflow, for the *entire* context of the chapter is about money. God sent Jesus to redeem us from the curse of the Law because He wants us to be rich.

We must understand that Jesus is not the remedy. We don't "get Jesus" in place of money.

When your car is broken, the mechanic is the solution, but the answer is a working car. You would call the mechanic crazy if he said to you, "Alright, I'm here now. I'm all you need." You'd say, "Uh, no. I need a working car."

In the same way, Jesus is the solution who gives us the answer.

God did not send Jesus to be a mechanic who sits with people while their life is broken and falling apart. God sent Jesus to redeem the world. Jesus is the solution to sin, and He gave us righteousness. He is the solution to poverty, and He gave us prosperity.

Religion relegates Jesus to the answer. People will say, "Oh, you're suffering. Here's Jesus. He'll hold your hand. He'll be with you through this time." The problem is no one actually gets redeemed—exactly why God sent Jesus!

On earth, Jesus changed situations. He calmed storms, not stopped them. He healed the sick, not recommended them to doctors. The same is true with regard to prosperity.

## THE LOVE OF MONEY

People ask, "I thought money was the root of all evil?" That's a misquote from scripture. The Bible actually says, **"For the LOVE OF MONEY is the root OF ALL KINDS OF EVIL. Some people, eager for money, have wandered from the faith and pierced themselves with many sorrows"** (1 Timothy 6:10). Money is not the problem, the love of money is the problem. And the love of money isn't even the root of all evil, it's the root of all kinds of evil. People simply have this whole theology wrong. God is not opposed to His children being wealthy, He is opposed to His children being covetous.

This was the issue with the rich man who Jesus encountered in Mark 10. Jesus did not condemn the man for being rich. Verse 21 even says that **"Jesus looked at him and loved him."** The issue ended up being that the rich man loved money more than God. He did not want to give. He was covetous. The love of money made him a hoarder and lover of possessions.

There is a difference between the pursuit of riches and the blessing of God. The love of money is the pursuit of materialism which results in destruction; the blessing of God comes from the pursuit of God, which results in blessing.

The distinction between the two is found all through scripture. For example, in Deuteronomy 8, God warned the Israelites who were promised immense wealth (Deuteronomy 28) not to allow the riches they were about to receive to turn their hearts from Him. Having God's financial blessing wasn't sinful, developing materialism would be sinful.

The book of Proverbs itself is full of this distinction. For example, Proverbs 10:22 reads, **"The blessing of the LORD brings wealth"** and then Proverbs 28:20 reads, **"but one eager to get rich will not go unpunished"** (Proverbs 28:20). It's not that God is flip-floppy or double-minded. It's that there's a difference between His blessing which produces wealth and being covetous.

Jesus' teachings on money reflect this, as well. For instance, in Matthew 6:33 Jesus said, **"But seek first his kingdom and his righteousness, and all these things will be given to you as well."** The key is loving God, then everything else that other people are striving to get will be given to you: clothes, money, food, cars, houses, etc.

If the rich man in Mark 10 would have obeyed Jesus' instruction and gave his possessions, he would have obtained the blessing of the

Lord as well—and in an even greater measure of wealth that he currently had! After he walked away sad, Jesus went on to tell His disciples:

**"'Truly I tell you,' Jesus replied, 'no one who has left home or brothers or sisters or mother or father or children or fields for me and the gospel will fail to receive a HUNDRED TIMES AS MUCH in this present age: homes, brothers, sisters, mothers, children and fields—along with persecutions—and in the age to come eternal life.'"**

Mark 10:29-30

He could have had 100 times as much if he would've let go of his love for money!

And more importantly, the love of money cost him his soul. As Jesus said, **"Children, how hard it is to enter the kingdom of God! It is easier for a camel to go through the eye of a needle than for someone who is rich to enter the kingdom of God"** (Mark 10:24-25).

One might then ask, "If it's so hard to enter heaven with riches, how then are we supposed to make it to heaven if God's blessing includes riches?"

Jesus told us the answer. He went on to say, **"With man this is impossible, but not with God; all things are possible with God"** (Mark 10:27). I understand that people quote this scripture for all sorts of things. They'll quote it going through a struggle. They'll quote it if they're attempting to set a world record at jumping cars on a motorcycle. But the context of the scripture is actually about rich people making it to heaven. Jesus is saying that with God the rich *can* make it to heaven. How? By seeking His kingdom first and pushing away materialism, yet ending up with wealth anyways because they love God and put Him first.

## GIVING OPENS GOD'S FINANCIAL BLESSING

Just because we are a Christian does not mean we are automatically guaranteed to be blessed financially. There is something we must do.

That is why there are some Christians who remain dirt poor and others who go from being dirt poor to owning businesses. God does not sovereignly choose who to make poor and who to make rich. He does not sovereignly prevent the poor from becoming rich and force the rich to become corrupt.

Where we end up in life is a result of our choices. God says in Deuteronomy 30:19-20, **"This day I call the heavens and the earth as witnesses against you that I have set before you life and death, blessings and curses. Now choose life, so that you and your children may live and that you may love the Lord your God, listen to his voice, and hold fast to him."** It may have been our parents' choice to do drugs which is why we are born poor, but we still have the ability through the power of God to rise beyond poverty and inherit His blessing by choices *we* make. God said above, **"Choose life"**—He wants us and has empowered us to choose.

Understanding and obeying what the Word says about prosperity is what takes Christians out of poverty and into wealth. It's not that prosperous Christians love God more than Christians who stay poor, but that they learned and applied something from the Bible the others have yet to learn and do. As Jesus said, it's those who *hear* and *do*: **"Therefore everyone who hears these words of mine and puts them into practice is like a wise man who built his house on the rock"** (Matthew 7:24). It would be an insult to Christ, then, to say that those who don't hear and don't do His Word can reap the same results as those who do.

What must we do? Giving is what God has instructed us to do in His Word to access His financial blessing. There are several types of giving mentioned in the Bible, such as tithes, first fruits, sowing seeds of increase, alms, sacrificial and honoring a prophet or minister. For the sake of time, we will address two of the most debated in the church today, tithes and sowing seeds:

**The Tithe**

To tithe means to give God a tenth of our income. The word tithe literally means tenth.

Abraham was the first individual in the Bible to tithe. In Hebrews 7, the Bible says that he tithed—or gave a tenth of the plunder—to Melchizedek.

Why did Abraham do this? We're told that it was because of how great this Melchizedek was (Hebrews 7:4). Tithing was a gift of honor.

The significance here is that Melchizedek is a type and shadow of Jesus. If Abraham tithed to the *type* of Jesus, how much more ought we to honor the actual Jesus by tithing? As the Bible says, those who are Abraham's children ought to do what he did (John 8:39, Galatians 3:29).

How do we tithe to Jesus? Hebrews 7:8 says that Jesus collects the tithe when it's given to the local church today: **"In the one case, the tenth is collected by people who die; but in the other case, by him who is declared to be living."** When we tithe to our church, we are tithing to Jesus.

Sadly, there are groups of believers that do not believe tithing is for today. They say it ended with the Old Testament because it was a part of the Law. What they don't understand is that tithing wasn't birthed out of an instruction from God under the Law, tithing was birthed as a gift of honor apart from the Law. To be against tithing would be against honoring Christ in all His greatness.

By setting ourselves against tithing, we set ourselves against the blessing that accompanies it. After Abraham tithed, God appeared to him once again and blessed him (Genesis 15).

Every instance of tithing in scripture involves a blessing that is linked to it. In Malachi 3:10, God gives a general description of the blessing which falls on all who tithe:

**"Bring the whole tithe into the storehouse, that there may be food in my house. Test me in this," says the Lord Almighty, "and see if I will not throw open the floodgates of heaven and pour out so much blessing that there will not be room enough to store it."**

How much is in the floodgates of heaven? More than we have room for!

I have been tithing ever since I started working, and I can honestly say that I have never been in a time of need. I have always had more than enough. I received so many scholarships and grants—some of which had nothing to do with GPAs—that I made money going to college. My wife and I bought our first home when I was only 20 and she was 19. We bought our first rental properties when I was 24. And we gave our first five-figure offering when I was 25. God has immensely blessed me just as He said He would through tithing.

There's also a second portion to this blessing: protection. Malachi 3:11 (KJV) says, **"And I will rebuke the devourer for your sakes..."** For Israel, this meant a protection over their crops from destructive insects and diseases. In other words, it meant that He will rebuke what tries to destroy their livelihood.

Recently, the furnace in our home broke. After having it inspected by an HVAC technician, we were told we would have to get a completely new furnace—a cost of about $2,200.00. Since we were saving up to buy a new vehicle, we did not have the money to just throw that away on a furnace.

Instead of panicking or getting angry at the Lord like many people do when something bad happens, my wife and I took a stand on God's Word. We prayed, "We thank you, Father, that you're good and that you promised you would provide for tithers and rebuke the devourer. So we thank you that you're going to work this whole situation out." We weren't sure yet how it was going to work out, but we know our God so we didn't worry.

A couple hours later, my wife received a call from an aunt who she rarely sees or talks to. The aunt said to my wife, "I'm not sure why I called you, but I was thinking about you—so how are you?"

After talking for a few minutes, her aunt asked about visiting our home, so my wife explained to her our heating situation. To that, her aunt said, "Oh, well I know a nice guy who owns a heating and cooling business. He's a Christian. I'll have him give you a call."

Upon inspecting our furnace, he said that he would get us the part we need for free! God rebuked the devourer! What was originally going to steal $2,200 from us was cut off! Praise God!

God will do the same for you when you tithe! The Bible says that **"God is no respecter of persons"** (Acts 10:34 KJV). In other words, what He will do for one, He will do for all. He doesn't love me more than He loves you. He is willing to be true to His Word for me just as much as He is willing to be true to His Word for you.

**Sowing Seeds of Increase**

When we give beyond the tithe to the Kingdom of God, the Bible calls such giving an "offering" or "sowing seeds." Read 2 Corinthians 9:6-7. We are to give, or sow seeds, just as we have decided in our heart. It can be any amount given to the local church above our tithe or a gift sown into another ministry.

The result of this giving is also financial blessing or increase:

**"And God is able to BLESS YOU ABUNDANTLY, so that in all things at all times, having all that you need, you will abound in every good work…Now he who supplies seed to the sower and bread for food will also SUPPLY AND INCREASE YOUR STORE OF SEED and will enlarge the harvest of your righteousness. You will be ENRICHED IN EVERY WAY so that you can be generous on every occasion, and through us your generosity will result in thanksgiving to God."**

2 Corinthians 9:8-11

Three different times we're told that by our sowing seeds into the Kingdom of God, we will see an increase and abundance in our seeds (our finances).

People say, "We don't give to get." But God says when we give we will get. The promise is literally, when you give, you will get. The promise is there not so we can ignore it and pretend like it isn't there, but so that we can do what it says. The promise is intended to produce action toward it—specifically, to make us givers. The scripture said, **"he who supplies seed to the sower,"** not seed to the eater or seed to the keeper.

Therefore, those who do not sow will not and cannot receive an increase or have an abundance in their finances. That's not even how God designed the natural law of sowing and reaping to function. One has to plant the seed to get more seeds. He cannot eat the seed and expect to get more seeds.

Moreover, that is not how God designed the spiritual act of giving to function. Galatians 6:7 tells us that God will not have it,

He will not be mocked, that we *will* reap what we sow. He supplies seed to those who give. So if we're not seeing an abundant supply of resources in our lives, we need to examine ourselves in this area of giving.

God is looking for givers. Why? For one, God Himself is a giver (John 3:16). Two, because it takes money to do things. It takes money to make an impact in the world for the Kingdom of God. It takes money to evangelize, care for the homeless, widows and orphans, build churches, hold outreaches in our communities, etc.

As Jesus explained in the parable of the talents (Matthew 25:14-30), when God finds someone who will advance His cause, He wants to bless that person with even more. In fact, Jesus demonstrated that God will take from those who *don't* give, and give to those who have and gave the most. He doesn't have a problem with His children being wealthy because His children promote His cause.

When my wife and I gave $750 at church to help a woman in need of rent money, little did we know that hours later her landlord would offer us to purchase that very property and three others—and at nearly half the market value! We sowed a seed into the Kingdom and reaped increase in our finances. We were taken to another level. And because of the increase, we've been able to help other families and give more toward evangelism.

This is what God desires for every believer. Become a giver. Advance the Kingdom of God by sowing seeds into ministry and you are guaranteed to see increase in your life.

## MAKE MONEY A TOOL

Becoming a giver as God desires essentially turns money into a tool to be used to advance the Kingdom of God. In turn, it prevents us from developing a "love of money" because we keep money in our hands (where one holds a tool) instead of in our hearts. When it's in our hearts, it's for selfish reason and ambition. When it's in our hands, it's for Kingdom advancement.

It's important for us to be wealthy and make money a weapon because when all the wealth is in the hands of sinners, the agenda of Satan is accomplished. Casinos, bars and strip clubs are built. Evil politics are financed. Greed and dishonest gain flourish. Such things ruin families, businesses and entire countries.

But this does not have to be the case. Proverbs 13:22 tells us, **"a sinner's wealth is stored up for the righteous."** God desires money to be in the hands of the righteous where they can push His agenda on the earth and run Satan out of business, literally.

The question is, how do we become givers? How do we break the love of money and make it become our weapon instead of our poison? The following truths, when grasped and followed, will ensure we keep money in our hands where it belongs:

**Love God**

Loving God is the first and master of all the points in making wealth be a tool in our lives. If we can develop a sincere, ever-increasing love for Him, we will be big givers. All the other points will eventually fall in line.

When I bought my wife her engagement ring, no one had to tell me to buy the most expensive ring I could afford. In fact, my family told me to buy one less expensive. Why? Because I love her.

In the same way, when we cultivate a love for the Lord, we will automatically give to Him—that is, to His Kingdom work. We won't need to be told to give, we will give out of love for Him, His Church and the lost.

The Bible marks David as a man after God's own heart (1 Samuel 13:14). It is no coincidence to discover, then, that David was a tremendous giver to God's Kingdom work. In 1 Chronicles 29, we read where David gave a massive offering to the Lord. David said:

**"Besides, in my devotion to the temple of my God I now give my personal treasures of gold and silver for the temple of my God, over and above everything I have provided for this holy temple: three thousand talents of gold (gold of Ophir) and seven thousand talents of refined silver...Now, who is willing to consecrate themselves to the Lord today?"**

1 Chronicles 29:3-5

At today's valuation of gold and silver, that amounts to over $4 billion! What an offering!

No one forced David to give that size of an offering to the Lord. And notice how easy it was for David in comparison to the rich man in Mark 10. Love for God and His Kingdom made all the difference!

It enabled David to use His money as a tool, to build the temple and advance God's work. David didn't withhold giving; love for God drove him to give.

The Apostle Paul also links our giving to love for the Lord. He wrote:

**"But since you excel in everything—in faith, in speech, in knowledge, in complete earnestness and in the love we have kindled in you—see that you also excel in this grace of giving. I am not commanding you, but I want to test the sincerity of your love…"**

2 Corinthians 8 :7-8

If we want to excel in giving, keep money out of our hearts and receive the Lord's blessing on our lives, we must cultivate a love for the Lord! He must become first priority in our lives.

**Understand Your Calling**

When it comes to finances, most people only quote the scriptures about God's desire that we be content. While that's true, that's only half the story.

In the name of love for God, religion often selfish-izes contentment. People say, "I have enough. I don't need to make a bunch of money to be happy. I'm comfortable making $45k a year." Notice the number of "I's" when people talk like that. And notice the lack of concern for others.

We're called to be Kingdom minded, people minded! We might be able to live on $60k a year, but imagine how much more we could do for the Kingdom of God if we made $100k or even a million! Wow!

This reality goes back to the blessing of Abraham and our inheritance of such blessing as outlined in Galatians 3. God told Abraham: **"...I will bless you and make you famous, and you will be a blessing to others"** (Genesis 12:2 NLT). That can't happen if we're poor—which is exactly why Abraham's blessing, and ours, included riches. Riches makes us liberators in the realms of finances.

When money is viewed through this lens of our calling, it becomes a lot more important. Having an abundance means being able to give, which means more souls. The more money, the more souls we can reach. So if money isn't important, souls aren't important because it takes money to reach souls. American Airlines won't let missionaries ride for free. FedEx doesn't fly packages of food to foreign countries for free. Stadiums and civic centers don't let you hold gospel crusades for free even though it's about Jesus.

Scriptural contentment, then, isn't about preventing people from becoming wealthy. The purpose of contentment is to center our focus on godliness—which is living for God's Kingdom work. 1 Timothy 6:6-9 tells us:

**"But godliness with contentment is great gain. For we brought nothing into the world, and we can take nothing out of it. But if we have food and clothing, we will be content with that.**

**Those who want to get rich fall into temptation and a trap and into many foolish and harmful desires that plunge people into ruin and destruction."**

Paul's point in being content isn't so that we won't be rich. The point in being content is so that we push away the love for money on the basis of godliness. As we said above, that means fulfilling our calling to be liberators.

Paul was writing to address a problem, the problem being a love for money. Godliness with contentment is bless-able (Proverbs 10:22). Godliness without contentment is not bless-able (Proverbs 21:17). This was the issue Paul needed to fix.

Content without godliness produces selfishness, where our only concern is our own needs and bashing everyone that makes more money than us to make us feel more religious. It does not produce liberators.

Contentment with a firm understanding of our calling is what godliness is all about, and it produces people who use wealth to advance the Kingdom of God: build churches, raise orphanages, finance missionaries and evangelists, fund local outreaches, even influence the political realm.

So when we read scriptures such as Proverbs 30:8-9 which reads, **"…give me neither poverty nor riches, but give me only my daily bread. Otherwise, I may have too much and disown you and say, 'Who is the Lord?' Or I may become poor and steal, and so dishonor the name of my God,"** we have to read them through the entire biblical context that the *love* of money is the problem. The point is to avoid covetousness, not money. Otherwise, a whole lot of Bible characters would be in trouble for having insane riches.

If we keep our calling at the forefront of our minds, we ensure that we'll keep money as a tool. It is there to advance our mission. That's not to say we won't see God's blessing in our lives, but that we won't develop a love for money that prevents us from having His blessing.

**Guard Your Mouth**

In Mark 10, Jesus assured us that whatever we give up for the Kingdom, God acknowledges what we've done by blessing us with 100 times as much as we left behind. That includes blessing in this age, or while we are on earth, not only once we are in heaven.

I've heard people say, "I left a great six-figure salary to go into the ministry and now I'm broke." They act as if they are better than God, that they bested God on being good and that He isn't going to pay them back. Nonsense!

Christians who speak like that will soon find themselves broke and won't have any significant money, not because God isn't a blesser but because of their mouths.

In Malachi 3:13-18, there were some Israelites who were speaking against God in this way. They were calling the sinners blessed and prospering, and claimed that the people of God were suffering. But God explained that it was because of how they were speaking against Him that they were lacking, and that those who honored Him with their words would be blessed.

God is not a harsh taskmaster and He isn't pleased when we speak of Him that way. Doing so actually pushes away His blessing.

This is what Jesus explains in The Parable of the Ten Minas. The servant who did not multiply the master's money considered his master a hard man, so he was afraid to multiply it. But in response, the master took away what mina the servant did have, and he said: **"I will judge you BY YOUR OWN WORDS, you wicked servant! You knew, did you, that I am a hard man, taking out what I did not put in, and reaping what I did not sow"** (Luke 19:22). Notice the sarcasm is the master's voice. How the servant thought and spoke of his master was what dictated how the master responded. It was the cause of him missing out on the increase the other servants received.

True faith in God calls God good, a blesser. Hebrews 11:6 says, **"And without faith it is impossible to please God, because anyone who comes to him must believe that he exists and that he rewards those who earnestly seek him."** Believing He rewards is just as vital as believing He exists.

We can be a tither and giver, but if we're speaking arrogantly against God and His blessing, we'll unfortunately find ourselves lacking His blessing.

Commit to placing a guard over your mouth. That means only speak good things about God, developing a faith-filled confession about money.

Declare God as your shepherd. As David said, **"The Lord is my shepherd, I lack nothing"** (Psalm 23:1). Thank Him that it is impossible for you to lack. He always provides for you with plenty left over to share with others (2 Corinthians 9:8).

Declare you are debt free and shall never be in debt again. Deuteronomy 28:12 assures you of this reality. Declare you are a lender, not a borrower.

It does not matter what is in your bank account. God who is your Father owns all the silver and all the gold (Haggai 2:8). Thank Him that He's ordered the transaction from His account to yours and that you'll see it in no time.

*CHAPTER 7*

# UNDERSTANDING JOB AND THE GOODNESS OF GOD

One of the most common questions people have when talking about the victory of the believer is, "What about Job?" For example, I will say to someone, "God wants to heal you." In response they ask, "Well, what about Job? Job was sick. His family was even killed."

To them, Job is viewed as a confusing contradiction to the rest of the Bible. They will say, "I believe in healing but sometimes things happen, like with Job." But that's like saying, "sometimes we sin, like David with Bathsheba." And besides, what "happens to us" isn't the same thing as how we should respond. In other words, just because Job suffered doesn't mean we have to suffer. That's why we're called Christians not Jobians. Our life is meant to look like Jesus' not like Job's. We are called to be liberators; we're not called to be people in need of being liberated.

Have you noticed that most of the teachings about Job center on relating to his suffering—not his prosperity, not his righteousness, not his restoration? Why is that? Why don't people say: "I'm righteous like Job" or "I'm extremely wealthy like Job" or even "I suffered like Job but now I'm two-times better off"? Because as we know Job didn't only suffer—everything he lost was restored and he received twice as much blessing as he originally had. You see, Satan wants people to relate to suffering so that he can complete his mission of destroying them (John 10:10).

Teachings that center on Job's suffering produce believers who have a twisted view of the goodness of God. They struggle with doubt their whole lives and never rise to be liberators to their generation. They are filled with questions and doubt, not faith.

In this chapter, we want to correct the interpretation of Job to be through the lens of our covenant with Jesus. Whereas traditionally the Book of Job has been used to dictate what the rest of the Bible means, proper hermeneutics instructs us to use the rest of the Bible to discern the story of Job and extract correct doctrine. Since the entire storyline of the Bible leads up to and hinges on Jesus, this requires a fixed focus on Jesus through Job's story. Even as we stated in the introduction of this book, because Jesus is the author and our perfecter of our faith, every question about God's will for the life of the believer must be answered through Him.

## YOU ARE NOT JOB

If we're going to relate to anyone in the Bible, the best "person" we can relate to is Jesus. He's the highest bar, our perfect example. There is value and lessons in the lives of Job, David, Moses, Peter and Paul, yes, but at the end of the day our utmost example to follow is Jesus. Relating to others, limiting ourselves to others, is less than. So when suffering, why do so many excuse themselves and their situations to be like Job when they *could* choose to compare themselves to Jesus? Why not say, "I'm going to be healed because Jesus healed people" instead of saying, "I'm like Job so I'm bound to suffer for a season." Choose the better example!

Hebrews 8:6 (NLT) says, **"But now Jesus, our High Priest, has been given a ministry that is FAR SUPERIOR to the old priesthood, for he is the one who mediates for us a FAR BETTER covenant with God, based on BETTER promises."** What happened to Job is *true*, but since we are under a better covenant, not all of his story is *truth* for us today. Although we may face similar attacks from Satan, how we are protected and the power we have to do something about it are incomparable to what Job had available.

Think of the difference between us and Job like the difference between walking and driving a car. One driving a car is not subject to the elements in the same way as one who must walk. They both go through the rain, but the driver stays dry. They both go through the heat, but the driver stays cool. So it would be nonsense to try to equate the journey of the one driving the car to the one who walked. Likewise, because of our better covenant, it is nonsense to teach that how we face hardship will inevitably be how Job faced it.

In what ways is our covenant better? See the following three ways:

For one, Job was under a covenant that was without a mediator between him and God. Job cried out in Job 9:33, **"If only there was**

**someone to mediate between us, someone to bring us together."**

When the law of Moses was given, priests functioned as the mediator between God and the people. So if Job would have lived after the Mosaic covenant was given, he would have had a priest which communicated to God on his behalf. However, there is not even a mention of the Levitical priesthood, the tabernacle or the Law in the entire book of Job. Our best conclusion then is that Job lived before the Law and did not have a priest who could mediate requests between him and the Lord. While Job served as a type of priest over his own family (Job 1:5) similar to Noah or Abraham, his "priesthood" was apparently limited in terms of communication with God (Job 13:3, Job 23:3-9). Obviously, he could not communicate with God like we can today.

Job was absent of a mediator, but our mediator is Jesus Himself! Jesus said regarding our covenant, **"In that day you will no longer ask me anything. Very truly I tell you, my Father will give you whatever you ask in my name"** (John 16:23). When we pray to the Father in Jesus' name, Jesus mediates with the Father on our behalf to get every prayer answered! What a blessing we now have!

Second, Job had only *heard* of God. Job said, **"I had only heard about you before, but now I have seen you with my own eyes"** (Job 42:5 NLT). He had never heard God speak, unlike how Noah, Abraham, Isaac or others even before the Law had. He had only heard about God from others. He did not have a *personal* revelation from God, which also meant he did not have a revelation of Satan, the Adversary. And perhaps this why he thought God was the one taking from him (Job 1:20)! *Therefore, Job did not have clear revelation on God's will.* That is why he later repents. As he said, **"...Surely I spoke of things I did not understand..."** (Job 42:3).

Today, we have the ability to personally hear the voice of the Holy Spirit and understand God's will. We have the Bible which is quite literally God's very words to us (2 Timothy 3:16). It is His revealed will for our lives. On top of that we have the Holy Spirit living inside us who leads us into *all* truth (John 16:13) and enables us to access even the deep things of God (1 Corinthians 2).

Third, because Job lived before the sacrifice of Jesus, he did not have the blessings that Jesus purchased for us with His blood. Job was not a "new creature" as described in 2 Corinthians 5:17. He did not have the power of sin broken over his life like we who believe in Jesus do. Job did not have the stripes of Jesus for healing as we do (1 Peter 2:24). Job had no covenant protection or blessings over his finances, unlike we who have Jesus (2 Corinthians 8:9).

## CONFUSION ABOUT THE GOODNESS OF GOD

Perhaps the main reason why people find it so easy to relate to Job is that like Job they are confused about the goodness of God. They believe that God orchestrates sickness and calamity in their lives.

Since Job didn't have a personal revelation about God, we could give him an excuse for his confusion about God's goodness. But believers today have no excuse since we have the Word of God and the Holy Spirit to teach us and speak to us.

**Who is the Oppressor?**

Job thought that God was the cause of his sickness, financial ruin and death of his children. Most famously he said, **"the Lord gave, and the Lord has taken away"** (Job 1:21) and **"Though he slay me, yet will I trust him"** (Job 13:15 KJV). In fact, Job blamed God time and time again for his suffering: Job 2:10, Job 6:4, Job 7:19-20, Job 9:17-18, Job 9:30-31, Job 9:34, Job 10:8, Job 12:9, Job 13:15, Job 16:11-14 and Job 19:6, etc. The Dake Annotated Reference Bible lists 74 different times Job charged God with wrongdoing.

If you've been around Christianity for any length of time, I would almost guarantee that you've heard a believer repeat one of these very things. I have heard them repeated and taught in sermons and they are frequently used lyrics in Christian radio.

*However, Job was wrong.* Job was attacked by Satan. It was not the Lord who took from Him.

First, notice the similarities between the description of Satan in Job's story and the description of Satan the New Testament:

**"One day the angels came to present themselves before the Lord, and SATAN also came with them."**

Job 1:6

According to the footnotes in the NIV as well as in the more literal Bible translations, Satan here means "adversary."

**"your ADVERSARY the devil…"**

1 Peter 5:8

Don't miss it! God is not called Job's adversary, Satan is called Job's adversary. God spoke well of Job (Job 1:8). God was the one who blessed and protected him (Job 1:9). God was the one who restored Job to even greater fortune (Job 42:10). Those are not things an adversary does. That's because Satan was his adversary.

Second, by comparing New Testament scriptures that highlight behavior, we can deduce that Satan presented himself before the Lord with the *intention* to devour someone:

**"The Lord said to Satan, 'Where have you come from?' Satan answered the Lord, "From ROAMING THROUGHOUT THE EARTH, going back and forth on it."**

Job 1:7

**"Be alert and of sober mind. Your enemy the devil PROWLS AROUND like a roaring lion looking for someone to devour."**

1 Peter 5:8

In both descriptions, the behavior of Satan is one of prowling. 1 Peter 5:8 adds, he prowls to destroy. That is why God asked Satan, **"Have you considered my servant Job?"** (Job 1:8). Satan was already prowling about considering someone to devour. This was not news to God. He knew that Satan attacked people. God was merely saying, "Did you notice Job while you were down there walking around? He's great. I love him." You could say God was actually bragging on him, expecting Job to be able to handle it.

Third, the Bible explicitly states that it was the devil's own hand that struck Job. Job 2:7 says, **"So SATAN went out from the presence of the Lord and afflicted Job with painful sores from the soles of his feet to the crown of his head."** It was not God giving Job sickness or taking from him. It was quite literally Satan, the adversary.

People say things like, "One day in eternity, God will make it clear why Christians suffer." It's not a mystery! We have an adversary called Satan whose will is to destroy people's live. He is the one causing people to suffer!

This description of Satan as the adversary is a constant throughout scripture. Ephesians 6:12 says the devil is a prince of darkness. 2 Corinthians 11:4 tells us he is a deceiver. Romans 12:10 calls him an accuser of God's people. In Matthew 13:19 he is the wicked one. In Matthew 13:39 he is the enemy of the Church. In Acts 10:38 he is called an oppressor. John 8:44 calls him a murderer. Let it get into your spirit that Satan is the oppressor and refuse to blame God! God is good; Satan is bad.

**What God Allows**

In response, someone may say, "Okay, but God *allowed* Satan to attack Job." Well, of course. God has repeatedly stated throughout the course of the entire Bible that there is an adversary who is allowed to attack people. That's why we're to pray God's will be done on earth as it is in heaven. His will isn't done on earth, believers have to co-labor with God to see it done. God's will is for healing, blessing and peace for people but because God's will is not done on earth, those things don't happen as our adversary is permitted to run about.

As we explained earlier in this book, what God allows has nothing to do with His will. God *wills* for all people to be saved (2 Peter 3:9), yet He *allows* people to choose hell (Deuteronomy 30:19, John 5:40). God *wills* for no one to be murdered (Romans 13:9), yet people are murdered every day.

We cannot get stuck on what's been allowed to attack us. We have to find God's will, grab hold of it and take our stand against Satan's schemes to have what God says we can have.

In fact, the Bible says that God allows what we allow and binds what we bind (Matthew 16:19, Matthew 18:18). What this means is that we have to resist Satan in order for him to flee. God isn't going to resist the devil for us, we have to resist the devil. God expects us to have faith in His good will for our lives and cause it to come to pass.

So if bad things happen in our lives, we don't just have to hold on for dear life. We aren't to just sit and wait it out while God allows this "season" in our life. Jesus never ministered that way. He didn't tell the sick or blind to just hang in there. He didn't say to the crippled, "God is most satisfied in you when you are most satisfied in Him so just learn to live with it." No! In every instance, Jesus healed people and set them free of oppression. He proclaimed to everyone that this year was God's year of favor for them (Luke 4:19). It is your time of favor, too!

James 5 teaches that we are to admire Job's perseverance—for Job ultimately refused to curse God and die. *Yet James goes on* to give us very specific instructions about what to do when we're in trouble so we don't just sit there and "hold on," trying not to give up on God like Job had to (because of his ignorance and lack of covenant). We're told to have patience like Job, but we're also told:

**"Is anyone among you in trouble? Let them pray. Is anyone happy? Let them sing songs of praise. Is anyone among you sick? Let them call the elders of the church to pray over them and anoint them with oil in the name of the Lord. And the prayer offered in faith will make the sick person well; the Lord will raise them up. If they have sinned, they will be forgiven. Therefore confess your sins to each other and pray for each other so that you may be healed. The prayer of a righteous person is powerful and effective."**

James 5:13-16

Clearly, we don't just sit around and let it happen. We're given clear instructions about what to do. Job however did not have that scripture. But thank God we do! We have the ability to pray which produces great power. We do not have to accept any trouble as our lot in life, for not only is it not of God, we have power from God to resist it and see victory in our lives!

**Do Not Be Deceived**

James 1:16-17 says, **"DON'T BE DECEIVED, my dear brothers and sisters. Every good and perfect gift is from above, coming down from the Father of the heavenly lights, who does not change like shifting shadows."** Who would have us be deceived about the goodness of God? The devil, of course. John 8:44 tells us that Satan is **"a liar and the father of lies."** The devil causes evil and destruction in our lives and then tries to get us to think it's God's doing in order to destroy our faith and to make us angry at God so we stop serving Him. That's why I am asked questions all the time such as, "If God is so good, why did *this* happen?" They're salty at God because they think He had some hand in what happened to them.

And since Job believed that God was his oppressor, it makes sense then that Job got to the point where he wanted to give up and die (Job 6:11-13, Job 7:16, Job 9:21, Job 9:29, Job 17:13, etc.). I mean if GOD is against you, you're a dead man. So no wonder he felt that way. He only saw the Redeemer from afar off, after his death (Job 19:25-26). He had no hope for his present life.

On the contrary, David said, **"I had fainted, unless I had believed to see the goodness of the Lord in the land of the living"** (KJV). David believed that he *would* see God's goodness in this life, which empowered him to continue living and not waiver in faith. In Psalm 23:6, David even said, **"Surely your goodness and love will follow me ALL THE DAYS of my life…"**

Like David we can be confident that God will always be good to us in our lives! The KJV words the verse in James 1:16-17: **"with whom there is no variableness, neither shadow of turning."** A shadow of turning refers to how the sun shines on a sundial throughout the day causing the shadow to turn. This means that God is like the sun on a fixed point. He's constant, unchanging in what He does. Every good and perfect gift comes from Him—nothing bad—that is His fixed point.

**God Gives Good Gifts**

In Matthew 7, Jesus teaches His disciples about the goodness of God and the types of gifts He gives. Notice the parallel Jesus makes between how both people and God perceive good and bad gifts.

**"You parents—if your children ask for a loaf of bread, do you give them a stone instead? Or if they ask for a fish, do you give them a snake? Of course not! So if you sinful people know how to give good gifts to your children, how much more will your heavenly Father give good gifts to those who ask him."**

Matthew 7:9-11 NLT

If even evil parents can discern that sickness, poverty and suffering are evil, how much more does the Lord understand that those things are bad! No good parent would cause harm to their child and neither will the Lord. Such a parent would be thrown in prison!

Could you imagine a guidance counselor or police officer telling a child whose father abuses them: "You must accept good from your father, and trouble"? Yet that was the theology Job was living by (Job 2:10) and what the modern church has been telling believers! They have said that "God is Good" includes that sometimes the Lord does bad things to us, whether we understand why or not, and we just have to accept it. And that we still have to call God "good." My friend, that is not good!

That's why the Bible says, **"Give thanks to the Lord, for he is good"** (Psalm 106:1), and not "Give thanks to the Lord, even if He isn't good." Bad gifts do not come from a good giver.

Scripture is packed full of specific examples of God's goodness and the gifts He gives:

Psalm 103:2-5 says, **"May I never forget the good things he does for me. He forgives all my sins and heals all my diseases. He redeems me from death and crowns me with love and tender mercies. He fills my life with good things"** (NLT). "Good things" does not stop with forgiveness but includes healing and a satisfying life!

In another place God tells us, **"I will rejoice in doing them good and will assuredly plant them in this land with all my heart and soul"** (Jeremiah 32:41). Observe the depth of His passion to do good to us—it's with all His heart and soul!

Similarly, Jesus tells us, **"Do not be afraid, little flock, for your Father has been pleased to give you the kingdom"** (Luke 12:32 NIV). The context of the passage and of "the kingdom" here is material things like homes, clothes and money. God is pleased to give us access to all of His kingdom resources!

So while many are begging God to do them good, thinking sometimes He simply doesn't desire to heal or deliver us, God is saying, "I will! I love to!"

Jesus, who is the exact representation of God's character and will (Hebrews 1:3), did not go around taking people's health or lives. If God were a taker of health, Jesus would have done so while alive on earth because Jesus came only to do the will of the Father. However, Matthew 8:17 tells us, **"This was to fulfill what was spoken through the prophet Isaiah: 'He took up our infirmities and bore our diseases.'"** The only thing Jesus took was sickness and disease, poverty and sin—all curses!

1 Samuel 2:6-9 (KJV) tells us:

**The Lord killeth, and maketh alive: he bringeth down to the grave, and bringeth up.**

**The Lord maketh poor, and maketh rich: he bringeth low, and lifteth up.**

**He raiseth up the poor out of the dust, and lifteth up the beggar from the dunghill, to set them among princes, and to make them inherit the throne of glory: for the pillars of the earth are the Lord's, and he hath set the world upon them.**

**He will keep the feet of his saints, and the wicked shall be silent in darkness; for by strength shall no man prevail.**

God does kill, make poor, bring down, and even make blind, deaf and mute (Exodus 4:11). But who in the Bible is it that God does such things to? The only people God ever "slays" in the Bible are evil people and those who come against His children. There is not a single instance in scripture where He destroys or makes sick His children—not a single one! From Israel driving out wicked nations (Deuteronomy 9:5) to Israel's various captivity to other nations (Ezekiel 39:23), and to those in the New Testament such as Elymas the sorcerer (Acts 13:8-11) and Ananias and Sapphira (Acts 5), every instance where someone is struck down by the Lord is because they either sinned or came against the Lord's children.

Psalm 146:6-9 tells us:

**He upholds the cause of the oppressed**
    **and gives food to the hungry.**
**The Lord sets prisoners free,**
    **the Lord gives sight to the blind,**
**the Lord lifts up those who are bowed down,**
    **the Lord loves the righteous.**
**The Lord watches over the foreigner**
    **and sustains the fatherless and the widow,**
    **but he frustrates the ways of the wicked.**

God is in the business of giving good gifts to people. God is in the business of keeping His saints and exalting them to places of honor, not destroying them. He does not wish any would sin and perish (2 Peter 3:9). It's His will to give good gifts to all of His creation (Psalm 145:9).

## A MATTER OF FAITH

Even though Job existed two covenants ago, he was not completely powerless to do something about his situation. From the beginning of humanity, the kingdom of God has always worked by faith. Abraham, Isaac, Jacob, Joseph, etc. all operated by faith and dominated in life over their oppressors.

The problem was that Job was not "in faith" when he got attacked. He was in fear. By his own admission, Job said, **"What I feared has come upon me; what I dreaded has happened to me"** (Job 3:25). When we are in fear, we are not in faith. For fear is doubt.

In Ephesians 6:16, Paul describes faith as a shield. He says, **"In addition to all this, take up the shield of faith, with which you can extinguish all the flaming arrows of the evil one."** When we are operating by faith, we walk through life as if carrying a shield before us which has the power to *extinguish* all the attack arrows of Satan. So in the presence of an attack, one says:

"I will live, I will not die."

"That sickness is not mine, healing is mine."

"My leaves shall stay vital and green even in this economic time of heat and drought."

"Satan, your arrows are extinguished! God's blessing is mine!"

Their faith is up so when they are attacked, they won't be hurt or hindered. Instead, they'll see the miraculous power that follows our faith in God. For faith can move mountains and makes all things possible (Mark 9:23).

Since Job was operating in fear instead of in faith for victory, he was shield-less. There was nothing he could do to extinguish the darts flying toward him and his family. All he could do was take shots and hope for the best.

People who do not have faith in the goodness and promises of God do not have any protection. All they can do is just take a hit and hope it's not too bad. If you listen to people, that's how they talk. They just hope the doctor can find a cure. They just hope their savings will be able to last through the recession. They have no faith to extinguish fiery darts in their lives.

If Job would have been operating in faith, his story could have looked much different. For example, Abraham believed in God's goodness very strongly. He prayed for healing *before* God ever revealed himself as Healer or before a healing covenant was given (Genesis 20:17). He knew God was that good. So why didn't Job do that? He could have easily believed in God's goodness just like Abraham and prayed for healing for himself and received it! But Job wasn't in faith.

Or, for example, with regard to Job's children dying, Abraham believed God could raise the dead (Hebrews 11:19). Why didn't Job? He could have just as easily like Abraham spoke in dead-raising faith to see his children raised back to life! But Job wasn't in faith.

Faith is the key to every victory in life! When we live in faith in the goodness of God and His promises, we live with a shield in front of us that puts all of Satan's arrows to naught. He may shoot them, but we extinguish them and remain standing as victors and liberators (Ephesians 6:13)!

*CHAPTER 8*

# LESSONS FROM JOB

In the previous chapter, we discussed that we do not have to be Job so we do not have to suffer like Job. Not only are we called to be like Christ—rather than called to be like Job—we have the ability to have faith in the goodness of God to see victory in our lives.

As we begin understanding Job through a "Jesus lens," we realize that we shouldn't even necessarily *want* to be Job. While Job certainly did some things right, much of what Job said and did was wrong, or at least ignorant. For this reason I tell people Job is more about what we should not do rather than what we should do.

We are not bashing or condemning Job by saying this. Rather, we are recognizing that the Bible contains progressive revelation. The Bible speaks of mysteries in God that were kept hidden in ages past, but have now been revealed (Colossians 1:26). There are things we know and have now that those in the Old Testament did not know or have. Some prophets and servants of God could see these new things from afar, but they did not have them (Hebrews 11:13, Matthew 13:17). Therefore, we must carefully discern what we can learn from these ancients, and in this case, from Job.

In this chapter, we will breakdown what Job did wrong and what we ought to say and do instead. Then, we will breakdown what Job did right so that we can repeat what he did in those areas.

## WHAT JOB DID WRONG AND WHAT TO DO INSTEAD

Beginning in Job 32 to the last chapter, Job gets rebuked. He gets rebuked by Elihu—the only person in the story of Job who *doesn't* get rebuked, which means his words are approved by God—for multiple chapters. And immediately after Elihu, Job gets rebuked by God Himself for several more chapters. Since he was rebuked, we can then conclude that this means Job did not say and do everything correctly.

In Job 42, Job himself repents for how he was thinking, acting and for what he said about the Lord:

> **"I know that you can do all things; no purpose of yours can be thwarted. You asked, 'Who is this that obscures my plans without knowledge?' Surely I spoke of things I did not understand, things too wonderful for me to know.**
>
> **"You said, 'Listen now, and I will speak; I will question you, and you shall answer me.' My ears had heard of you but now my eyes have seen you. Therefore I despise myself and repent in dust and ashes."**
>
> Job 42:2-6

The New American Standard Bible (NASB) and some of the other more literal translations translate verse 6 differently, saying, **"Therefore I retract, And I repent in dust and ashes."** A word study reveals that the Hebrew word *'em-'as* more frequently means "I retract" rather than "I despise myself."

A combination of both word meanings is likely the most correct interpretation, catching Job's meaning through his emotion, which could be said like this: I despise myself for what I said and take it back. This is probably why the NLT translates it: **"I take back everything I said, and I sit in dust and ashes to show my repentance."**

An understanding and acknowledgement of Job's rebuke and repentance is vital because we should not repeat the same things and have the same attitude that caused someone else to have to repent. And since the majority of the record we have of Job contains things he said that he took back, this is especially true.

Again, the intent here isn't to bash Job but to learn from his mistakes like we do everyone else in the Bible. For example, we know not to commit adultery even though King David committed adultery with Bathsheba. Or, for example, we know not to doubt Jesus even though Thomas stubbornly doubted Jesus' resurrection.

If we ignore the reality that Job got rebuked and had to repent, we are bound to make the same mistakes he made. And if we make the same mistakes as Job, we will unfortunately find ourselves repenting just as Job did.

So then, let us identify the things Job said or did wrong that we can learn from:

**Job Accused God of Wrongdoing**

At first, immediately after suffering, Job did not accuse God of wrongdoing. He worshipped. The Bible records:

**"At this, Job got up and tore his robe and shaved his head. Then he fell to the ground in worship and said:**

**'Naked I came from my mother's womb,
   and naked I will depart.
The Lord gave and the Lord has taken away;
   may the name of the Lord be praised.'**

**In all this, Job did not sin by charging God with wrongdoing."**

Job 1:20-22

Instead of the word "wrongdoing," some other translations use the word "blame." Based on the progression of Job's attitude toward the Lord which we'll explain in a moment, I believe "wrongdoing" is the correct word usage.

Word choice is important here because there is a difference between blaming God and accusing God of wrongdoing. You can blame someone for something without accusing them of wrongdoing. For example, if someone crashes their car into your car, it is their fault. You can blame them. But it doesn't mean that the person crashed into yours on purpose—which would be wrongdoing.

The reason why Job is said to have not sinned by saying these things about God is because Job was blaming God from a heart of innocence, not accusing the Lord of wrongdoing. He was not attacking God. He was not harboring hatred toward God. He did not think the Lord did anything to him that was outside of what He was rightful to do. So even though Job was factually wrong about his oppressor, for we know that Satan was the one who smote Job (Job 2:7), Job was spiritually in the right.

However, Job *did* go on to accuse God of wrongdoing:

> "For he attacks me with a storm and repeatedly wounds me without cause."
>
> Job 9:17

> "…then know that God has wronged me and drawn his net around me."
>
> Job 19:6

> "Then Elihu said:
> Do you think this is just? You say, 'I am in the right, not God.'"
>
> Job 35:1-2

Why the shift in Job's attitude? It shifted *after* he sat in silence and sadness for seven straight days (Job 2:13). While he sat there sadly, something was apparently taking place in his thought-life that changed his attitude toward the Lord, because the first words out of his mouth after the seven days were over were curses (Job 3:1).

We don't simply just develop a hostile attitude toward the Lord. Our attitude is largely shaped by our thoughts. What we allow ourselves to dwell on, whether good or bad, will ultimately have an effect on what we say and how we act.

In fact, one of Satan's methods of destruction is by attacking the mind. 2 Corinthians 10:4-5 (KJV) says: **"(For the weapons of our warfare are not carnal, but mighty through God to the pulling down of strong holds;) Casting down imaginations, and every high thing that exalteth itself against the knowledge of God, and bringing into captivity every thought to the obedience of Christ;"** Even Eve was attacked in her mind—in her understanding of God's Word (Genesis 3:1).

The key in winning the battle of the mind, in taking thoughts captive instead of being captive to them, is joy. The Bible says, **"the joy of the Lord is your strength"** (Nehemiah 8:10 NLT). Joy gives us the strength in both our spirits and minds to fight the attacks on our minds. Our thought-life will remain strong, and we will maintain a positive, hopeful, "in faith" spirit man.

An absence of joy causes a state of weakness in spirit and in thought. That's why sulking or depressed people are typically doubters who question the existence or goodness of God. They haven't taken the time to strengthen themselves in the Lord's joy, so they don't have the spiritual stamina necessary to resist the thoughts Satan has sent against their mind. Instead, they dwell on the questions and feelings Satan stirs in them—that they are not worthy, that God has forgotten about them or even that God has deceived them, as in the case of Eve.

Because the shift in Job's attitude happened after a period of silence and sadness, I believe that he allowed himself to dip into a level of sadness that took a toll on his thought-life and ultimately spiritual well-being. He was lacking the joy of the Lord, so he lacked strength to maintain a strong spirit-man and mind.

In order to stay in joy and in the strength of the Lord, we must do a few things:

First, we must increase our consumption of the Word. Jeremiah 15:26 (NLT) says, **"When I discovered your words, I devoured them. They are my joy and my heart's delight, for I bear your name, O Lord God of Heaven's Armies."** He ate God's Words and discovered they were full of joy.

God's words contain joy-giving nutrients. As we discover them and eat them, joy is absorbed into our spirits. The more we chew on them, pondering on the meaning and depths of His Words, the more we nourish and strengthen ourselves with joy!

Second, we must increase our communion with the Holy Spirit. By praying in the Spirit, we build ourselves up in the Spirit's strength for Christian living (Jude 1:20). Since one of the fruit of the Holy Spirit is joy, this means being built up in the joy of the Lord. As Romans 14:17 says, **"For the kingdom of God is not a matter of eating and drinking, but of righteousness, peace and joy in the Holy Spirit."** We can't pray in the Holy Spirit every day and remain sad. It's impossible! When we contact the Spirit, we reap joy!

Third, we need to surround ourselves with people who will encourage us, reminding us of God's faithfulness and our identity in Him as anointed liberators in Christ! As the Bible says:

**"See to it, brothers and sisters, that none of you has a sinful, unbelieving heart that turns away from the living God. But ENCOURAGE ONE ANOTHER DAILY, as long as it is called 'Today,' so that none of you may be hardened by sin's deceitfulness. We have come to share in Christ, if indeed we hold our original conviction firmly to the very end."**

Hebrews 3:12-14

Don't let, "I don't have any encouraging friends" be an excuse. We need to locate a Spirit-filled church and get involved. Move to a different state if necessary. God will honor you as you put Him first (Matthew 6:23, 1 Samuel 2:30).

Just because someone is a believer doesn't mean they are an encourager. Job's three friends were not encouragers. They were pity-ers and condemners. They sat in silence with him instead of encouraging him. And then once Job did speak, the only thing they did was condemn him.

Believers who empathize with others, apologizing for how bad they have it do no good, either. Jesus didn't empathize with people. He had compassion on them but then ministered by the anointing (Matthew 14:14, Matthew 20:34) to deliver them. So an encourager is one who ultimately leads that person to freedom, not who comforts you through bad times.

Elihu was an encourager. His response to Job was faith-filled. He reminded Job, **"Far be it from God to do evil, for the Almighty to do wrong. He repays everyone for what they have done; he brings on them what their conduct deserves. It is unthinkable that God would do wrong, that the Almighty would pervert justice"** (Job 34:10-12).

So the qualification of a good encourager in the Lord is someone who will say, "far be it from God to do evil." It is someone who talks about the goodness of God! Commit to surrounding yourself with that kind of person and you'll have more joy fused into your spirit than you know what to do with!

### Job Complained

In scriptures such as Job 3:1-26, Job 6:1-3, Job 6:5-6, Job 7:15-16, Job 10:1, Job 10:18, etc. we read that Job complained during his suffering. He even admitted to his complaining during a few of his speeches (Job 21:4).

While we can certainly understand why Job complained, because of the severity of his situation, complaining prevents us from accessing the power of God through praise and thanksgiving to liberate us and cause victory in our lives. In every instance in the Bible, complainers live in defeat, while thankful people inherit and live in victory.

For example, when the Israelites sent 12 men to spy on the land of Canaan, 10 out of the 12 spies brought back a negative report to the rest of the Israelite people. They said that they should not try to attack and possess the land, for the people living there were giants and too strong for them. The problem was that God had already promised them that it was theirs, that they could take the land!

Unfortunately, the rest of the Israelites believed and agreed with the report of the 10 spies and started complaining against God. The Bible says they started grumbling against Moses and Aaron, their leaders, and started saying that it would have been better if they died in the wilderness than be where they are now (Number 14:2-4).

In response, God said:

**"How long will this wicked community grumble against me? I have heard the complaints of these grumbling Israelites. So tell them, 'As surely as I live, declares the Lord, I will do to you the very thing I heard you say: In this wilderness your bodies will fall—every one of you twenty years old or more who was counted in the census and who has grumbled against me. Not one of you will enter the land I swore with uplifted hand to make your home, except Caleb son of Jephunneh and Joshua son of Nun."**

Numbers 14:27-30

It wasn't God who defeated them, it was their own words. God promised them complete victory. He was on their side. But it was how they spoke that determined what they would actually receive, which was complaining against God's promises and saying they'd rather die.

People like to complain and talk however they want and then cry,

"Grace." It's not as if God wasn't gracious in the Old Testament in terms of how people spoke, and then here in the New Testament He decided to be a "nice guy." No, God doesn't change. He was just as gracious then as He is now. What we say now, even though under the covenant of Christ, still matters. If our words are powerful enough to be involved in the miracle of salvation (Romans 10:10), then they are powerful enough to direct the course of our life and dictate whether or not we receive God's other blessings of healing, salvation and victory.

When we speak in thankfulness and praise, we see victory and increase in our lives! Jeremiah 30:19 (KJV) says, **"Then out of them shall proceed thanksgiving and the voice of those who make merry; I will multiply them, and they shall not diminish; I will glorify them, and they shall not be small."**

God blesses people who are thankful. That's why the Bible says, **"Be thankful in all circumstances, for this is God's will for you who belong to Christ Jesus"** (1 Thessalonians 5:18 NLT). It's not because God wants to "change our perspective" about our situation, it's because God wants to liberate and bless us. If we're thankful in every circumstance, we will always see blessing.

At one time, I held a secular job at a construction company. The owner of the company was very abrasive, to say the least. On several occasions, he stormed into my office and literally screamed at me at the top his voice over problems he thought were my fault, even though they weren't. When I say several occasions, I mean *several* occasions. It was to the point where I was considering getting a different job.

Instead of allowing me to complain about the situation, my wife encouraged me in the goodness of God (importance of being surrounded by encouragers as we discussed in the last section!) to thank and praise the Lord in order to see favor. So every day on my way to work, I would thank and praise Him: "Thank you for my job which allows me much free time to do ministry. You are such a good God! I thank you that I have favor with both God and man. I thank you that you have made my boss favorably disposed toward me as you did the Israelites and Egyptians."

Shortly after that, I decided to ask off for an additional week of vacation for a ministers and leaders conference in another state—even though I had already used my one allotted week of paid vacation. Sure enough, I was allowed to go and received my pay just as if I had been working!

Choose to speak only thanksgiving and praise! Even when the situation is bad, refuse to complain and praise the Lord and you can be sure to see His victory in your life! You won't stay in defeat, you'll praise your way to victory!

**Job Became Bitter**

In Job 7:11, Job said, **"Therefore I will not keep silent; I will speak out in the anguish of my spirit, I will complain in the bitterness of my soul."** Job allowed himself to become bitter.

Hebrews 12:15 warns us of the dangers of bitterness: **"See to it that no one falls short of the grace of God and that no bitter root grows up to cause trouble and defile many."** Bitterness, like a root, if allowed to remain will plant itself deeper into the soil of our heart and cause trouble in our lives.

Take tree roots, for example. If left unattended, they can cause detrimental damage to building foundations. Likewise, roots of bitterness will affect our foundation in Christ to the point that we are deemed condemned—or defiled—and fall short of God's grace.

For Job, his bitterness was a result of loss. But bitterness may also arise from bad relationships, betrayal, poor work experiences, failure, and many other things.

The only way to treat bitterness, because it is a root, is to pull it out and replace it with thankfulness That means letting go of whatever happened to us and turning our gaze fully back on the Lord in thankfulness.

Lamentations 3:17-24 tells us:

**"I have been deprived of peace; I have forgotten what prosperity is. So I say, 'My splendor is gone and all that I had hoped from the Lord.'**

**I remember my affliction and my wandering, the bitterness and the gall. I well remember them, and my soul is downcast within me. Yet this I call to mind and therefore I have hope:**

**Because of the Lord's great love we are not consumed, for his compassions never fail. They are new every morning; great is your faithfulness. I say to myself, 'The Lord is my portion; therefore I will wait for him.'**

The writer said, "Yet I call to mind…" He was undergoing the transition from a bitter spirit to a spirit of thankfulness for the Lord's faithfulness. He wasn't fully consumed, so he had a reason to be thankful and let go of the pain he endured.

Whatever may or may not have happened to us, we can destroy the root of bitterness by remembering that it's because of the Lord we weren't fully consumed by pain or hardship. We can raise our hands and thank God that He never fails!

Colossians 2:7 links thankfulness to an increase of faith. So as we let thankfulness take root in our hearts, we will increase in faith to see God's promises be fulfilled in our lives!

**Job was Arrogant**

Another mistake we can see in Job was that he developed an arrogant attitude toward serving God.

**"For he says, 'There is no profit in trying to please God.'"**

Job 34:9

**"Do you think this is just? You say, 'I am in the right, not God.' Yet you ask him, 'What profit is it to me, and what do I gain by not sinning?'"**

Job 35:1-3

In Malachi 3, we find that God himself calls saying these very type of things and this type of attitude arrogant:

"You have spoken arrogantly against me," says the Lord. Yet you ask, 'What have we said against you?' "You have said, 'It is futile to serve God. What do we gain by carrying out his requirements and going about like mourners before the Lord Almighty? But now we call the arrogant blessed. Certainly evildoers prosper, and even when they put God to the test, they get away with it.'"

Malachi 3:13-15

It is a slap in the face to God when we say there is no point in serving Him. He is our creator! He is a miracle worker! More than that, as the scripture says, **"for in him we live and move and have our being"** (Acts 17:28). We need God—He doesn't need us in the least. We have *everything* to gain by serving Him.

There was another group of people in Malachi 3 that honored the Lord with their words and attitudes:

"Then those who feared the Lord talked with each other, and the Lord listened and heard. A scroll of remembrance was written in his presence concerning those who feared the Lord and honored his name."

"On the day when I act," says the Lord Almighty, "they will be my treasured possession. I will spare them, just as a father has compassion and spares his son who serves him. And you will again see the distinction between the righteous and the wicked, between those who serve God and those who do not."

Malachi 3:16-18

So when we honor God with our thoughts and words, we attract God's blessings on our lives. He writes our names down to be sure that we get rewarded.

David said, **"May the words of my mouth and the meditation of my heart be pleasing to you, O Lord"** (Psalm 19:14 NLT). Let us put a guard over our mouths and minds so that we only bless the Lord with how we speak and our attitudes!

WHAT JOB DID RIGHT THAT WE SHOULD DO

Despite Job's mistakes and misunderstandings, there are some truths that we can pull from Job's story that are very applicable to our life today:

**Perseverance**

The one thing Job did right that is an example for us to follow is that he refused to curse God in suffering.

**"His wife said to him, 'Are you still maintaining your integrity? Curse God and die!'**

**He replied, 'You are talking like a foolish woman. Shall we accept good from God, and not trouble?'**

**In all this, Job did not sin in what he said."**

Job 2:9-10

The ultimate plan of the enemy in attacking Job and us is to get us to curse God. That's what the Bible means when it says thieves come to steal, kill *and* destroy. Destroy here means our salvation, our right-standing with the Lord.

But Job knew that cursing God was sheer foolishness. Although he made some harsh claims toward the Lord, he refused to give up on God despite all the death and pain that had taken place. He was able to persevere through his ordeal. As James 5:11 tells us, **"As you know, we count as blessed those who have persevered. You have heard of Job's perseverance and have seen what the Lord finally brought about. The Lord is full of compassion and mercy."**

Perseverance is integral to our faith as believers. Without perseverance we will just give up on God at the first sign of an attack of the enemy. Hebrews 10:36 says, **"You need to persevere so that when you have done the will of God, you will receive what he has promised."**

To persevere means to be strong. It's been said, "When the going gets tough, the tough get going." Quitters quit when it starts getting tough. But we're not called to be quitters, we're called to be strong. Ephesians 6:10 says, **"Finally, be strong in the Lord and in his mighty power."**

Being strong in the Lord doesn't mean sulking in your living room all alone with the blinds to your house pulled because you got a cancer diagnosis.

Being strong in the Lord doesn't mean drinking a few beers to ease the stress after a bad day.

Being strong in the Lord doesn't mean changing your theology simply because you prayed once and nothing happened.

Being strong in the Lord doesn't mean skipping out on church because you're frustrated about how things are going in your life.

However, being strong in the Lord does mean setting it firmly in your heart like Job did that no matter what happens you're in this for the long haul. Come hell or high water, you determine that you will serve God and you will see God's promises come about in your life!

**Accessing the Mercy of God**

In James 5:11, the Bible says, **"You have heard of Job's perseverance and have seen what the Lord finally brought about. The Lord is full of compassion and mercy."** Job was restored because of the mercy of God. However, it was not simply God's sovereign mercy, if you will, that manifested Job's restoration.

Jesus said in Matthew 5:7, **"Blessed are the merciful, for they will be shown mercy."** We access God's mercy as believers when we show others mercy.

This is what Job did. Job 42:10 says, **"After Job had prayed for his friends, the Lord restored his fortunes and gave him twice as much as he had before."** God was merciful not because He randomly or sovereignly decided Job had had enough but because Job was merciful. Job was shown mercy after he showed mercy. Job accessed God's mercy.

We can't walk in unforgiveness and expect God to bless us. In fact, in Mark 11 during one of Jesus' strongest teachings on the power of faith, Jesus says, **"And when you stand praying, if you hold anything against anyone, forgive them, so that your Father in heaven may forgive you your sins"** (Mark 11:25). Not even faith, even though it is powerful, can work if we are walking in unforgiveness.

But when we persist on being merciful, God will be merciful to us. We will access His goodness and blessings!

Forgive anyone who has done you wrong. Don't hesitate! Release them in your heart or physically approach them if you feel led by God to do so. As you do, you can trust the Lord that the blessing or turnaround you need is on its way.

*CHAPTER 9*

# UNDERSTANDING SUFFERING & PAUL'S THORN

The Bible says that we're to suffer for Christ: 1 Peter 1: 6-9, 1 Peter 3:13-17, 2 Timothy 2:3, Acts 14:22, Colossians 1:24, 2 Corinthians 1:3-11, 2 Corinthians 4:8-9. But what kind of "suffering" are we called to endure?

I have heard it preached that "suffering for Christ" means all sorts of things, including sickness, disease, loss, depression, financial hardship, even death of a loved one. But when we look honestly at scripture, that is not how it is defined. Suffering for Christ means suffering for the sake of the Gospel, which the Bible calls persecution.

When Paul lists his sufferings in 2 Corinthians 6, all of them are directly related to persecution. 1 Peter 3 is talking about persecution. Paul in Acts 1:24 is talking about being in prison. Paul continues in 2 Timothy 2 in verse 8-9, "as I preached my gospel, for which I am suffering, bound with chains as a criminal." In 2 Corinthians 1, the cause of suffering is again persecution for preaching the Gospel.

In Colossians 1 and 2 Corinthians 1, Paul calls suffering, "Christ's afflictions" and "sufferings of Christ." Likewise 1 Peter 2:20-21 says, "But if you suffer for doing good and you endure it, this is commendable before God. To this you were called, because Christ suffered for you, leaving you an example, that you should follow in his steps." We are called to suffer "like" Christ. How did Christ suffer? Persecution. He was "despised, rejected, a man of sorrows." Jesus wasn't sick. He didn't suffer with depression. So if Jesus' type of suffering didn't include any of those things, neither must ours.

The only way we can suffer "for Christ" would be if that suffering is "for" Him. How does suffering with sickness do anything *for* Jesus? How does it do anything for the advancement of the Gospel? When people are sick, they are at home, not preaching the Gospel. So if anything, sickness hinders us from doing something for Christ. Us being sick doesn't get people saved; the Gospel gets people saved. Being able to maintain a Christian witness through sickness before doctors and family, though good and holy, is nowhere called for in scripture. Christianity is about freeing the suffering, not about how much we can suffer through random hardships or loss in life.

No, suffering for Christ requires that we are suffering directly for participation in the advancement of the Gospel. As Paul said in 2 Timothy 2:8-9, it is the gospel for which he is suffering. In other words, he is putting up with being persecuted because he MUST preach about Jesus. People are trying to stop him and kill him, but he will continue to preach so people can be saved.

**Paul's Thorn**

One of the scriptures people use to teach that believers must suffer is Paul's thorn.

First, if Paul's thorn was sickness or some sort of suffering outside of persecution, this would be the only place in the Bible where this is so. And that is not how hermeneutics works. Hermeneutics teaches us not to base doctrine off of one scripture, but to use the rest of scripture to determine what one particular passage means. For this reason, Paul's thorn cannot be sickness or suffering.

Second, Jesus, who was the exact representation of God, who *only* did God's will, didn't give sickness to a single person for their spiritual betterment, let alone at all. Jesus is the same yesterday, today and forever. If He didn't give sickness during His earthly ministry, He's not going to change His ministry philosophy from heaven.

The only time in scripture God "gives" sickness, disaster or suffering is to His enemies. God struck the Egyptians with all sorts of plagues and sickness, He crumbled the walls of Jericho and empowered David to cut off Goliath's head—all examples of enemies of God. God used sickness and disaster to punish the Israelites when they were living in *sin,* of course, but not once in all of scripture does the Lord use sickness to develop people spiritually. If sickness is employed, if you will, it is always, always punishment for sin. So if someone wants to claim God is using sickness to teach them something, they'd also have to be admitting they did something to deserve punishment. But that's not how it works. God doesn't use sickness or suffering as a textbook in itself.

So what was Paul's thorn then? The only intellectually and scripturally honest conclusion we can come to was that it was persecution.

The metaphor of a "thorn" bothering people is used in other scriptures, and it is used to mean people—that people are the thorn:

> "But if you do not drive out the inhabitants of the land, those you allow to remain will become barbs in your eyes and **THORNS** in your sides. They will give you trouble in the land where you will live."
>
> Numbers 33:55

> "Therefore I also said, 'I will not drive them out before you; but they shall be **THORNS** in your side, and their gods shall be a snare to you.'"
>
> Judges 2:3 NKJV

> "then you may be sure that the LORD your God will no longer drive out these nations before you. Instead, they will become snares and traps for you, whips on your backs and **THORNS** in your eyes, until you perish from this good land, which the LORD your God has given you."
>
> Joshua 23:13

And you, son of man, do not be afraid of them or their words.

**Do not be afraid, though briers and THORNS are all around you and you live among scorpions. Do not be afraid of what they say or be terrified by them, though they are a rebellious people.**

Ezekiel 2:6

**"No longer will the people of Israel have malicious neighbors who are painful briers and sharp THORNS. Then they will know that I am the Sovereign LORD."**

Ezekiel 28:24

As we presented earlier, persecution is not only expected for believers but a must if we want to be like Jesus. It would be the one thing we could pray for to be taken away to which God would say "No."

## A FINAL WORD

You are called by God to follow in the footsteps of Jesus to be a liberator. Acts 1:1 says, **"In my former book, Theophilus, I wrote about all that Jesus BEGAN to do and to teach."** What Jesus BEGAN you are called to FINISH. It's our responsibility as believers to continue Jesus' work until He comes. And He's coming soon!

I don't believe we're living in the last days, I believe we're living in the *final hours* of the last days. When you're in the last minutes of the last quarter of a ball game, you don't take it easy, you go even harder. When you're in the last stretch of a race, you don't slow down or pace yourself, you run even harder and even faster. In 1 Corinthians 9:24 NLT, Paul says, **"Don't you realize that in a race everyone runs, but only one person gets the prize? So run to win!"** Run to win. Run after Jesus with everything that you have! Get a spiritual violence about you, plunder hell and populate heaven. REFUSE to allow any oppression from Satan to remain on your life. Get free. And then go and get others free. Be a liberator. Don't just talk about Jesus, *really* live like Jesus—it's your covenant obligation! Demonstrate the love and power of God with signs following.

I see you stepping into a new level, in Jesus' name! I see you carrying a strong anointing of the Holy Spirit, in Jesus' name. I see you healing the sick and raising the dead, in Jesus' name. I see you leading thousands of souls to Jesus. You'll do it, in Jesus' name! Go. Be the liberator God has called you to be.

# ENDNOTES

1. Gee, Donald. *Concerning Spiritual Gifts*. Springfield, MO: Gospel Publishing House, Revised 1980.

2. Bosworth, F.F. (Fred Francis) *Christ the Healer*. Grand Rapids, MI: Baker Publishing Group, Revised 2000.

3. Kenyon, E.W. *Two Kinds of Faith*. Kenyons Gospel Publishing, 1989.

4. raphaelsoares360. "The Unlimited God – T. L. Osborn." YouTube, YouTube, 4 Nov. 2013, www.youtube.com/watch?v=wgcDMQitMqU.

5. Oyedepo, David. *Exploits in Ministry*. Canaan Land, Ota: Dominion Publishing House, 2006.

www.ingramcontent.com/pod-product-compliance
Lightning Source LLC
Chambersburg PA
CBHW060154050426
42446CB00013B/2823